An Explanation

of

Luther's Small Catechism

1992

Warren Olsen
David Rinden
Editors

Faith and Fellowship Press

Box 655
Fergus Falls, Minnesota 56538-0655

An Explanation of Luther's Small Catechism, 2nd Edition

Scripture text, unless otherwise indicated, taken from the *Holy Bible, New International Version.* Copyright © 1973, 1978, 1984 International Bible Society. Used by permission of Zondervan Bible Publishers.

Art work by Lynn Sunwall.

ISBN 0-943167-20-5

Printed in the United States of America.

Contents

Dedication 4

Preface 5

Introduction 9

Ten Commandments 15

First Table of the Law 18

The First Commandment 18

The Second Commandment 20

The Third Commandment 23

Second Table of the Law 25

The Fourth Commandment 26

The Fifth Commandment 28

The Sixth Commandment 30

The Seventh Commandment 34

The Eighth Commandment 36

The Ninth Commandment 39

The Tenth Commandment 41

Conclusion 43

The Three Articles of the Creed 49

The First Article — Creation 53

The Second Article — Redemption 60

The Third Article — Sanctification 75

The Lord's Prayer 99

The First Petition 103

The Second Petition 105

The Third Petition 108

The Fourth Petition 110

The Fifth Petition 112

The Sixth Petition 114

The Seventh Petition 118

Conclusion 118

The Sacraments 123

The Sacrament of Baptism 123

The Sacrament of the Lord's Supper 132

Conclusion 136

Scripture Index 139

Subject Index 145

Dedication

This Explanation of Luther's Small Catechism

is dedicated to

the memory of

Dr. Erik Pontoppidan

Lutheran Pastor

Who in 1737 wrote

An Explanation of Luther's Small Catechism

Upon which this Explanation is based.

Preface

Since the time of the Reformation, Martin Luther's Small Catechism has been one of the texts used to instruct the church, and
especially its young people, in the teachings of the Bible. As the word
catechism suggests, Luther's *Small Catechism* is a book of questions
and answers.

This present *Explanation of Luther's Small Catechism* is one of many
published since Martin Luther first compiled his catechism in 1529. It
is an attempt to provide a clear setting forth of Bible teaching for the
church in this generation.

It is based on one published by the Evangelical Lutheran Free Church
of Norway, which was translated into English in 1939 and revised
again twenty years later. These Explanations are all based on one
published in 1737 by Dr. Erik Pontoppidan, a Danish Lutheran pastor
and theologian who had a profound influence on congregational life
in the Scandinavian countries.

The task before the church in each generation is to explain the Bible
accurately and carefully to that generation. This *Explanation* is an attempt
to assist in this task. It is sent forth with the prayer to the Lord of the
Church that it will help many come to a clearer understanding of God's
way of salvation and lead to a living faith.

We hereby acknowledge with thanks the many pastors and lay-persons
who read the manuscript and provided useful comments and insights.
We are particularly indebted to the Rev. Everald H. Strom, the Rev.
Omar Gjerness, and the Rev. Eugene Boe.

The Editors

Introduction

1. What are God's thoughts about you?

God's thoughts about me are thoughts of love and blessing.
John 3:16 — *For God so loved the world that he gave his one and only Son, that whoever believes in him shall not perish but have eternal life.*
Psalm 139:17 — *How precious to me are your thoughts, O God! How vast is the sum of them!*

2. What is God's will for you?

God's will is that I be saved and come to the knowledge of the truth (I Timothy 2:3,4).
John 10:10 — *"The thief comes only to steal and kill and destroy; I have come that they may have life, and have it to the full."*

3. Where does God show us how we may be saved?

God shows us how we may be saved in His Holy Word, the Bible.
John 20:31 — *These [words] are written that you may believe that Jesus is the Christ, the Son of God, and that by believing you may have life in his name.*

4. How did God give the Bible to us?

God gave us His written word by inspiring chosen prophets, evangelists, and apostles, giving them the thoughts and words to write.
II Peter 1:21 — *For prophecy never had its origin in the will of man, but men spoke from God as they were carried along by the Holy Spirit.*
II Timothy 3:16 — *All Scripture is God-breathed and is useful for teaching, rebuking, correcting and training in righteousness...*
I Corinthians 2:13 — *This is what we speak, not in words taught us by human wisdom but in words taught by the Spirit, expressing spiritual truths in spiritual words.*

5. Does the Bible teach you everything necessary for salvation?

Yes, the Bible alone teaches the complete truth about salvation.
John 20:30,31 — *Jesus did many other miraculous signs in the presence of his disciples, which are not recorded in this book. But these are written that you may believe that Jesus is the Christ, the Son of God, and that by believing you may have life in his name.*
II Peter 1:3,4 — *His divine power has given us everything we need for life and godliness through our knowledge of him who called us by his own glory and goodness. Through these he has given us his very great and precious promises, so that through them you may participate in the divine nature and escape the corruption in the world caused by evil desires.*
See also John 5:24.

6. Is the Bible sometimes hard to understand?

The Bible is sometimes hard to understand, but it is clear enough to those who use it correctly.

7. How should you correctly use the Bible?

I should regularly read and hear it thoughtfully, asking the Holy Spirit to instruct me so that I can believe it and live according to its teaching.
John 16:13a — *But when he, the Spirit of truth, comes, he will guide you into all truth.*
Luke 11:28 — *Blessed...are those who hear the word of God and obey it.*

8. Why should you pray for help in understanding the Bible?

I should pray for help in understanding the Bible because my mind is darkened by sin, and I cannot understand it by myself.
I Corinthians 2:14 — *The man without the Spirit does not accept the things that come from the Spirit of God, for they are foolishness to him, and he cannot understand them, because they are spiritually discerned.*

9. What is the main truth of the Bible?

The main truth of the Bible is that Jesus is the only way of salvation.

John 14:6 — *Jesus answered, "I am the way and the truth and the life. No one comes to the Father except through me."*

Luke 24:45-49 — *Then he opened their minds so they could understand the Scriptures. He told them, "This is what is written: The Christ will suffer and rise from the dead on the third day, and repentance and forgiveness of sins will be preached in his name to all nations, beginning at Jerusalem. You are witnesses of these things. I am going to send you what my Father has promised; but stay in the city until you have been clothed with power from on high."*

10. What are the two main teachings of the Bible?

The two main teachings of the Bible are the Law and the Gospel.

11. What is the Law?

The Law is that teaching of the Word of God which tells me how I am to be and what I am to do and not to do.

Leviticus 19:2b — *"Be holy because I, the Lord your God, am holy."*

12. What is the Gospel?

The Gospel is the good news in which God tells me what He has done for me through Jesus Christ, especially in dying for my sin and rising in victory over death and Satan.

I Corinthians 15:1-5 — *Now, brothers, I want to remind you of the gospel I preached to you, which you received and on which you have taken your stand. By this gospel you are saved, if you hold firmly to the word I preached to you. Otherwise, you have believed in vain.*

For what I received I passed on to you as of first importance: that Christ died for our sins according to the Scriptures, that he was buried, that he was raised on the third day according to the Scriptures, and that he appeared to Peter, and then to the Twelve.

The Ten Commandments

13. How many kinds of law did God give?

God gave three kinds of law: 1) The ceremonial law; 2) The civil law; and 3) The moral law.

14. What were the ceremonial and civil laws?

The ceremonial and civil laws in the Old Testament showed the Hebrew people how they should worship God and how they should behave themselves in their tribes.

15. What is the moral law?

The moral law tells me about my duty toward God and my fellow human beings.

16. Which of these laws is still in effect?

The New Testament shows us that only the moral law is still binding. The ceremonial and civil laws no longer apply (Ephesians 2:14-18).
Hebrews 7:18,19 — *The former regulation is set aside because it was weak and useless (for the law made nothing perfect), and a better hope is introduced, by which we draw near to God.*

17. How has God revealed His moral law?

1. At the creation, God wrote His law in the human conscience (Romans 2:15).

2. At Mount Sinai He gave His law in the Ten Commandments, written on two tables of stone (Exodus 20:1-17). The first table of the law contains the first three commandments and tells of our relationship to God; the second table of the law contains the last seven commandments and tells of our relationship to others.

18. What does God demand of you in the law?

In the law, God demands that I be as pure and holy as He is in everything I think, in everything I say and in everything I do.
Luke 10:27 — *"Love the Lord your God with all your heart and with all your soul and with all your strength and with all your mind, and, Love your neighbor as yourself."*

19. Can you be saved through keeping the law?

No, I cannot be saved through keeping the law because since the Fall no human being has been able to keep God's Law perfectly.
Romans 3:23 — *...All have sinned and fall short of the glory of God...*
Galatians 2:16b — *So we, too, have put our faith in Christ Jesus that we may be justified by faith in Christ and not by observing the law, because by observing the law no one will be justified.*

20. Is the law, then, of any benefit?

Yes, God's law is of great benefit to me.
I Timothy 1:8 — *We know that the law is good if one uses it properly.*

21. What does the law do?

1. The law sets up a standard of moral values by which every human society is to be regulated and evil restrained.
Romans 3:20 — *Therefore no one will be declared righteous in his sight by observing the law; rather, through the law we become conscious of sin.*

2. The law shows me my sin and God's hatred of it, troubles my conscience, and shows me my need to seek Christ.
Galatians 3:24 — *The Law was in charge of us until Christ came, in order that we might then be put right with God through faith (Today's English Version).*

3. The law guides me on how I should live, after God by His Spirit has revealed Himself to me.

Psalm 119:105 — *Your word is a lamp to my feet and a light for my path.*

22. What should be your attitude toward the law?

Since the law shows me God's will, I should love it and follow it, even though I know Jesus has fully kept the law to give me salvation, and there is nothing more that I need to do to be saved.

23. What is the central teaching of the law?

The central teaching of the law is to love God and my neighbor. Matthew 22:37-40 — *Jesus replied: "Love the Lord your God with all your heart and with all your soul and with all your mind. This is the first and greatest commandment. And the second is like it: Love your neighbor as yourself. All the Law and the Prophets hang on these two commandments."*
See also Luke 10:27.

24. What two things do you need to remember as you study each commandment?

In each commandment I must remember the evil which God forbids and the good which He requires.

25. What did God say before He gave the Ten Commandments to Moses?

He said, "I am the Lord your God, who brought you out of Egypt, out of the land of slavery" (Exodus 20:2).

26. Why was this introduction given?

It was given to show that God loved His people and that He acted to help them in a particular time and place and that His action towards them was one of kindness.
Psalm 125:2 — *As the mountains surround Jerusalem, so the Lord surrounds his people both now and forever.*

The First Table of the Law

27. **What is the First Table of the Law and what does it teach?**

The First Table of the Law consists of the first three commandments. These teach us to love God.
Luke 10:27 — *"'Love the Lord your God with all your heart and with all your soul and with all your strength and with all your mind' and, 'Love your neighbor as yourself.'"*

The First Commandment

You shall have no other gods before me (Exodus 20:3).

What does this mean?

This means that we are to fear, love, and trust God above anything else.

28. **What does God forbid in the First Commandment?**

In the First Commandment God forbids me to put anyone or anything ahead of Him.

29. What do human beings sometimes worship instead of the One True God?

They sometimes worship: 1) Images made of wood and stone; 2) Created things such as the sun, moon, and stars; or 3) Anyone or anything placed ahead of the One True God.
Romans 1:21-23 — *For although they knew God, they neither glorified him as God nor gave thanks to him, but their thinking became futile and their foolish hearts were darkened. Although they claimed to be wise, they became fools and exchanged the glory of the immortal God for images made to look like mortal man and birds and animals and reptiles.*

30. What does God require in the First Commandment?

In the First Commandment God requires me to fear, love, and trust Him above all things.

31. What does it mean to fear God above all things?

To fear God above all things means that I honor Him so much that I will not offend Him by anything I think, say, or do.
Proverbs 8:13a — *To fear the Lord is to hate evil...*

32. What does it mean to love God above all things?

To love God above all things means that He is more dear to me than anything else and that I gladly do His will.
John 14:21a — *Whoever has my commands and obeys them, he is the one who loves me.*

33. What does it mean to trust God above all things?

To trust God above all things means I rely upon His promises with my whole heart; that I trust in Him to supply everything I need; and that I depend completely upon Him by placing all the details of my life in His hands.
Proverbs 3:5,6 — *Trust in the Lord with all your heart and lean not on your own understanding; in all your ways acknowledge him, and he will make your paths straight.*

Philippians 4:19 — *And my God will meet all your needs according to his glorious riches in Christ Jesus.*

34. Why should you respect, love, and trust God above all things?

I should respect, love, and trust God above all things because He alone is God and worthy of such respect, love, and trust.

The Second Commandment

You shall not misuse the name of the Lord your God, for the Lord will not hold anyone guiltless who misuses his name (Exodus 20:7).

What does this mean?

This means that we are to fear and love God so that we do not use His name to curse, swear, conjure, lie, or deceive, but call on Him in prayer, praise, and thanksgiving.

35. What do we mean by God's name in the Second Commandment?

By God's name in the Second Commandment we mean all the names given to Him in the Bible, each of which shows me something about who He is and what He does.

36. When is God's name misused?

God's name is misused whenever I do not show respect for it.

37. What does it mean to curse by God's name?

To curse by God's name is to ask God to damn someone or something.

38. What does it mean to swear by God's name?

To swear by God's name is to declare something to be true by God's name.

39. Does the Bible ever give permission to swear by God's name?

The Bible permits swearing when the proper authorities require an oath.
Deuteronomy 6:13 — *Fear the Lord your God, serve him only and take your oaths in his name.*

40. What must I remember when I am required to take an oath?

I must remember that God sees and hears everything and that I really am calling down God's judgment if I commit perjury and do not tell the whole truth.
Leviticus 19:12 — *Do not swear falsely by my name and so profane the name of your God. I am the Lord.*

41. What does it mean to conjure by God's name?

To conjure is through the devil's power or influence to use God's name to perform supernatural deeds. Other sinful practices included under conjuring are witchcraft, astrology, consulting spirits, and fortune telling.

42. What does it mean to lie and deceive by God's name?

A person can lie and deceive by God's name by perjury, teaching false doctrine, and hypocrisy.

Matthew 15:8,9 — *These people honor me with their lips, but their hearts are far from me. They worship me in vain; their teachings are but rules taught by men.*

43. What must I expect if I misuse the name of God?

If I misuse God's name, I must expect great punishment both in time and in eternity, for the Lord will not hold me guiltless if I misuse His name.

44. What should your speech be like as a Christian?

My speech should show respect for God's name and I should not use it or any form of it carelessly. Any careless use of God's name is to be avoided.

45. How does God want me to use His name?

God wants me to use His name with devotion and reverence, sincerely calling upon Him in every time of need and worshiping Him with prayer, praise, and thanksgiving.

Psalm 50:15 — *"...Call upon me in the day of trouble; I will deliver you, and you will honor me."*

Hebrews 13:15,16 — *Through Jesus, therefore, let us continually offer to God a sacrifice of praise — the fruit of lips that confess his name. And do not forget to do good and to share with others, for with such sacrifices God is pleased.*

Psalm 100:4 — *Enter his gates with thanksgiving and his courts with praise; give thanks to him and praise his name.*

The Third Commandment

Remember the Sabbath day by keeping it holy (Exodus 20:8).

What does this mean?

This means that we should fear and love God so that we do not despise His word and the preaching of it, but consider it to be holy and gladly hear and learn it.

46. What does the word Sabbath mean?

The word *Sabbath* means *rest.*

47. What does the word holy mean?

The word *holy* means *set apart to the service of God.*

48. What did God require of the Hebrew people in the Third Commandment?

God required them to keep the Sabbath Day holy.

49. What was the Sabbath Day for the Hebrew people in the Old Testament?

The Sabbath Day for the Hebrew people in the Old Testament was the seventh day of the week. This day was set apart for worshiping God and for rest.
Genesis 2:2 — *By the seventh day God had finished the work he had been doing; so on the seventh day he rested from all his work.*

Exodus 20:9-11 — *Six days you shall labor and do all your work, but the seventh day is a Sabbath to the Lord your God. On it you shall not do any work, neither you, nor your son or daughter, nor your manservant or maidservant, nor your animals, nor the alien within your gates.*

50. What day did the Christians in the New Testament set apart as a day to worship God and hear His Word?

Christians in the New Testament set apart Sunday, the first day of the week, the day when Christ arose from the dead and the day when the Holy Spirit was given.

51. Does Sunday replace the Sabbath Day of the Old Testament?

No, most Christians observe Sunday, the first day of the week, as a matter of free choice as did the early Christians, not in order to keep the law, but to rest their bodies and to have a set time to worship God and hear his Word.

Romans 14:5 — *One man considers one day more sacred than another; another man considers every day alike. Each one should be fully convinced in his own mind.*

52. What are some ways to observe Sunday?

I may observe Sunday by meeting for public worship, hearing God's Word, and receiving the Lord's Supper; by showing kindness to others; and by using this day to rest and renew myself.

Hebrews 10:25 — *Let us not give up meeting together, as some are in the habit of doing, but let us encourage one another — and all the more as you see the Day approaching.*

Romans 10:17 — *Consequently, faith comes from hearing the message, and the message is heard through the word of Christ.*

James 1:27 — *Religion that God our Father accepts as pure and faultless is this: to look after orphans and widows in their distress and to keep oneself from being polluted by the world.*

53. Are there other days which the church recognizes as being important?

Yes, the church considers as being important such days which mark events in the life of our Lord Jesus Christ in the time of His

Incarnation. Some of these days are: Advent Sunday, Christmas Day, Epiphany, Palm Sunday, Good Friday, Easter, Ascension Day, and Pentecost.

54. **How are these days arranged?**

These days are arranged in a calendar known as the Church Year which begins on Advent Sunday, four Sundays before Christmas.

The Second Table of the Law

55. **What is the Second Table of the Law and what does it teach?**

The Second Table of the Law consists of the last seven commandments. These commandments teach that I am to love my neighbor as myself.

56. **When do you love yourself in the right way?**

1. I love myself rightly when I realize that God loves me and that I am created in His image.
Psalm 139:13,14a — *For you created my inmost being; you knit me together in my mother's womb. I praise you because I am fearfully and wonderfully made...*
Psalm 8:3-9 — *When I consider your heavens, the work of your fingers, the moon and the stars, which you have set in place, what is man that you are mindful of him, the son of man that you care for him? You made him a little lower than the heavenly beings and crowned him with glory and honor. You made him ruler over the works of your hands; you put everything under his feet: all flocks and herds, and the beasts of the field, the birds of the air, and the fish of the sea, all that swim the paths of the seas. Oh Lord, our Lord, how majestic is your name in all the earth!*

2. I love myself rightly when I care for the salvation of my immortal soul and for my physical well-being.

Matthew 6:33 — *But seek first his kingdom and his righteousness, and all these things will be given to you as well.*
Matthew 16:26 — *What good will it be for a man if he gains the whole world, yet forfeits his soul? Or what can a man give in exchange for his soul?*

57. Who is your neighbor?

Everyone is my neighbor (Luke 10:25-37).

58. When do you love your neighbor in the right way?

I love my neighbor in the right way when I do what Jesus tells me to do when He said, "In everything, do to others what you would have them do to you..." (Matthew 7:12).
Matthew 5:44 — *But I tell you: Love your enemies and pray for those who persecute you...*
James 1:27 — *Religion that God our Father accepts as pure and faultless is this: to look after orphans and widows in their distress and to keep oneself from being polluted by the world.*

The Fourth Commandment

Honor your father and your mother, so that you may live long in the land the Lord your God is giving you (Exodus 20:12).

What does this mean?

This means that we should fear and love God so that we do not despise our parents and those in authority nor provoke them to anger, but honor, serve, obey, love, and think highly of them.

59. Why should you honor your father and your mother?

I should honor my father and mother because God has placed them over me to care for my physical, emotional, and spiritual welfare.

Ephesians 6:1-3 — *Children, obey your parents in the Lord, for this is right. "Honor your father and mother" — which is the first commandment with a promise — "that it may go well with you and that you may enjoy long life on the earth."*

60. What does it mean to honor your father and mother?

I honor my father and mother when I give them my respectful, loving, and willing obedience and faithfully serve them all my days.

Luke 2:51a — *Then he [Jesus] went down to Nazareth with them [Mary and Joseph] and was obedient to them.*

61. Whom should you honor besides your parents?

I should honor all those God has placed over me, such as guardians, employers, pastors, teachers, and government officials.

Hebrews 13:17 — *Obey your leaders and submit to their authority. They keep watch over you as men who must give an account. Obey them so that their work will be a joy, not a burden, for that would be of no advantage to you.*

62. Should you obey your parents or others in what is sinful?

No, in such cases I should obey God rather than people.

Acts 5:29 — *Peter and the other apostles replied: "We must obey God rather than men!..."*

Matthew 10:37 — *"Anyone who loves his father or mother more than me is not worthy of me; anyone who loves his son or daughter more than me is not worthy of me..."*

63. What should be your attitude toward your parents if they are divorced or separated?

I should still love them, try to understand them, and ask God to help me to honor them.

64. **When do you sin against the Fourth Commandment?**

I sin against the Fourth Commandment when I do not show my parents or those in authority over me proper respect and when I hurt them by disobedience, ingratitude, or by committing other sins.

65. **What is meant by the promise added to this commandment?**

The promise which is added to this commandment means that a special blessing rests upon obedient children and upon nations where parents and those in authority are honored.
Proverbs 14:34 — *Righteousness exalts a nation, but sin is a disgrace to any people.*

66. **Does this mean that anyone who dies young has been disobedient to parents?**

No, we are all part of a fallen world and share naturally in the evils that all human beings experience.

The Fifth Commandment

You shall not murder (Exodus 20:13).

What does this mean?

This means that we should fear and love God so that we do our neighbor no bodily harm nor cause any suffering, but help and befriend our neighbor in every bodily need.

67. How do you fail to keep the Fifth Commandment?

I fail to keep this commandment if I take my neighbor's life or if I hate or harm my neighbor in any way.

I John 3:15 — *Anyone who hates his brother is a murderer, and you know that no murderer has eternal life in him.*

68. How do you injure your neighbor in other ways?

I injure my neighbor when I cause him or her to sin, either by leading him or her astray or by being a bad example.

69. What does God require of you in the Fifth Commandment?

God requires in the Fifth Commandment that I help and befriend my neighbor in every need and treat that neighbor with love and kindness (Luke 10:25-37).

Hebrews 13:15-16 — *Through Jesus, therefore, let us continually offer to God a sacrifice of praise — the fruit of lips that confess his name. And do not forget to do good and to share with others, for with such sacrifices God is pleased.*

I John 3:16 — *This is how we know what love is: Jesus Christ laid down his life for us. And we ought to lay down our lives for our brothers.*

70. Does God forbid you to take your own life?

Yes, God has given me life, and He alone has the right to take it. If I take my own life, I commit murder.

71. How do you harm your health and shorten your life?

I can harm my health and shorten my life by laziness, neglect of my body, recklessness, overeating, drunkenness, chemical dependency, immoral sex, anger, and worry.

72. Is there ever a time when you should risk your health and life?

Yes, it may be necessary to risk my life to defend my country, carry out my occupation, save someone's life, or because of what I believe.

73. Why is human life sacred?

Human life is sacred because God is the one who from the moment of conception created my life.

Psalm 139:13-16 — *You made all the delicate, inner parts of my body, and knit them together in my mother's womb. Thank you for making me so wonderfully complex! It is amazing to think about. Your workmanship is marvelous — and how well I know it. You were there while I was being formed in utter seclusion! You saw me before I was born and scheduled each day of my life before I began to breathe. Every day was recorded in your Book! (The Living Bible).*

The Sixth Commandment

You shall not commit adultery (Exodus 20:14).

What does this mean?

This means that we should fear and love God so that we lead a chaste and pure life, in word and deed, and that husband and wife love and respect each other.

74. What does God require of you in the Sixth Commandment?

God requires that I live a chaste and pure life in thought, word, and deed, whether married or unmarried, and that husband and wife love and respect each other.

75. What is marriage?

Marriage is the lifelong union of one man and one woman who agree to enter into this relationship and promise to care for and be faithful to each other.

Matthew 19:4-6 — *"...At the beginning the Creator made them male and female, and said, For this reason a man will leave his father and mother and be united to his wife, and the two will become one flesh . . . So they are no longer two, but one. Therefore what God has joined together, let man not separate."*

76. Who instituted marriage?

God Himself instituted marriage at Creation and has given it His blessing.

Genesis 2:18 — *The Lord God said, "It is not good for the man to be alone. I will make a helper suitable for him."*

Genesis 1:27,28 — *So God created man in his own image, in the image of God he created him; male and female he created them. God blessed them and said to them, "Be fruitful and increase in number; fill the earth and subdue it . . ."*

77. How should husband and wife care for each other?

Husband and wife should care for each other by recognizing each other as a gift from God, should love and respect each other, and should stand by each other in good and evil days until death parts them.

Ephesians 5:23-25 — *For the husband is the head of the wife as Christ is the head of the church, his body, of which he is the Savior. Now as the church submits to Christ, so also wives should submit to their husbands in everything. Husbands, love your wives, just as Christ loved the church and gave himself up for her . . .*

I Thessalonians 4:3-8 — *For God wants you to be holy and pure, and to keep clear of all sexual sin so that each of you will marry in holiness and honor — not in lustful passion as the heathen do, in their ignorance of God and his ways.*

And this also is God's will: that you never cheat in this matter by taking another man's wife, because the Lord will punish you terribly for this, as we have solemnly told you before. For God has not called us to be dirty-minded and full of lust, but to be holy and clean. If anyone refuses to live by these rules he is not disobeying the rules of men but of God who gives his Holy Spirit to you (The Living Bible).

78. What should your attitude be toward divorce?

I should understand that God hates divorce and that His desire is that no marriage be broken.

I Corinthians 7:10,11 — *To the married I give this command (not I, but the Lord): A wife must not separate from her husband. But if she does, she must remain unmarried or else be reconciled to her husband. And a husband must not divorce his wife.*

Matthew 19:8,9 — *Jesus replied, "Moses permitted you to divorce your wives because your hearts were hard. But it was not this way from the beginning. I tell you that anyone who divorces his wife, except for marital unfaithfulness, and marries another woman commits adultery.*

79. Does God intend that everyone marry?

No, a person does not need to marry to live a life pleasing to God.

80. How is the Sixth Commandment broken?

1. The Sixth Commandment is broken when husband and wife are unfaithful to each other and their marriage vows.

Hebrews 13:4 — *Marriage should be honored by all, and the marriage bed kept pure, for God will judge the adulterer and all the sexually immoral.*

2. The Sixth Commandment is also broken when a person takes pleasure in impure thoughts, desires, language, and acts.

Ephesians 5:3 — *But among you there must not be even a hint of sexual immorality, or of any kind of impurity, or of greed, because these are improper for God's holy people.*

Matthew 5:27,28 — *"You have heard that it was said, Do not commit adultery. But I tell you that anyone who looks at a woman lustfully has already committed adultery with her in his heart."*

Ephesians 4:29 — *Do not let any unwholesome talk come out of your mouths, but only what is helpful for building others up according to their needs, that it may benefit those who listen.*

81. How can you avoid this sin?

I can avoid this sin with God's help:

1. By turning away from anything that will cause me to think impure thoughts or to lose control of my power to make right decisions.
II Timothy 2:22 — *Flee the evil desires of youth, and pursue righteousness, faith, love and peace, along with those who call on the Lord out of a pure heart.*

2. By thinking about the true purpose of my sexuality and the great blessing it can be when used in agreement with God's will.
Genesis 1:27 — . . . *God created man in his own image, in the image of God he created him; male and female he created them.*

3. By realizing that the pleasure of this sin is only for a short time and that it may have long-term evil consequences.
Hebrews 11:24,25 — *By faith Moses, when he had grown up, refused to be known as the son of Pharaoh's daughter. He chose to be mistreated along with the people of God rather than to enjoy the pleasures of sin for a short time.*

4. By remembering the great suffering that Jesus went through to save me from my sin.
Hebrews 12:3 — *Consider him who endured such opposition from sinful men, so that you will not grow weary and lose heart.*

82. Since you know temptations will come, how can you strengthen yourself?

I can use my will to say no to things I know to be wrong, and I can fill my mind with good thoughts, take part in healthful and creative activities, and do good things for my neighbors.
II Corinthians 10:5b — . . . *We take captive every thought to make it obedient to Christ.*
Philippians 4:8,9 — *Finally, brothers, whatever is true, whatever is noble, whatever is right, whatever is pure, whatever is lovely, whatever is admirable — if anything is excellent or praiseworthy — think about such things. Whatever you have learned or received or heard from me, or seen in me — put it into practice. And the God of peace will be with you.*

I Corinthians 15:33 — *Do not be misled: "Bad company corrupts good character."*

83. What help is there when you are tempted?

God has promised to be with me and give me His strength.
I Corinthians 10:13 — *No temptation has seized you except what is common to man. And God is faithful; he will not let you be tempted beyond what you can bear. But when you are tempted, he will also provide a way out so that you can stand up under it.*
Psalm 119:9,11 — *How can a young man keep his way pure? By living according to your word. I have hidden your word in my heart that I might not sin against you.*
Philippians 1:6 — *... Being confident of this, that he [God] who began a good work in you will carry it on to completion until the day of Christ Jesus.*
Philippians 2:13 — *... For it is God who works in you to will and to act according to his good purpose.*

The Seventh Commandment

You shall not steal (Exodus 20:15).

What does this mean?

This means that we should fear and love God so that we do not rob our neighbor of his money or property, nor bring them into our possession by unfair dealing or fraud, but help him to improve and protect his property and right to make a living.

84. Why has God given you this commandment?

God has given me this commandment so that both my neighbor and I may live free of the fear of having my possessions taken from me.

85. What is the source of money and possessions?

God gives me money and possessions through honest work, investment, discovery, gifts, and inheritance.
I Corinthians 10:26 — *"The earth is the Lord's and everything in it."*

86. How should you use money and possessions?

I should use my money and possessions as a faithful manager of the things God has given to me and remember that I am always accountable to Him.

87. What does it mean to steal?

1. I steal when I take even the smallest possession without the owner's permission or knowledge.

2. I steal when I hold back what may be due anyone.
Leviticus 19:13 — *Do not defraud your neighbor or rob him. Do not hold back the wages of a hired man overnight.*
James 5:4 — *Look! The wages you failed to pay the workmen who mowed your fields are crying out against you. The cries of the harvesters have reached the ears of the Lord Almighty.*

88. Is it wrong to be a partner of a thief?

Yes, the partner of a thief is no better than the thief because the partner is approving the act by being present and saying nothing.
Proverbs 29:24a — *The accomplice of a thief is his own enemy . . .*

89. What does God require of you in the Seventh Commandment?

God requires that I shall be honest and unselfish in all my actions, and that I help to improve and protect my neighbor's property and right to make a living.

I John 3:17 — *If anyone has material possessions and sees his brother in need but has no pity on him, how can the love of God be in him?*

Leviticus 25:35 — *If one of your countrymen becomes poor and is unable to support himself among you, help him as you would an alien or a temporary resident, so he can continue to live among you.*

Ephesians 4:28 — *He who has been stealing must steal no longer, but must work, doing something useful with his own hands, that he may have something to share with those in need.*

90. What should be your attitude toward money and possessions?

I should pray, "... give me neither poverty nor riches, but give me only my daily bread. Otherwise, I may have too much and disown you and say, Who is the Lord? Or I may become poor and steal, and so dishonor the name of God" (Proverbs 30:8,9).

Luke 12:15 — *Then he [Jesus] said to them, "Watch out! Be on your guard against all kinds of greed; a man's life does not consist in the abundance of his possessions."*

The Eighth Commandment

10ᵗʰ Dec.

You shall not give false testimony against your neighbor (Exodus 20:16).

What does this mean?

This means that we should fear and love God so that we do not misrepresent, betray, lie about, nor slander our neighbor, but defend him, speak well of him, and say the kindest things we can about all he does.

91. **What is a false testimony?**

I give a false testimony when I speak unkindly and untruthfully about my neighbor in a court of law or in my daily life.

92. **How is a false testimony given in a court of law?**

1. A false testimony is given when a witness testifies to a lie, withholds the truth, or makes a false charge.
Proverbs 19:5 — *A false witness will not go unpunished, and he who pours out lies will not go free.*
Proverbs 25:18 — *Like a club or a sword or a sharp arrow is the man who gives false testimony against his neighbor.*

2. A false testimony is given when a person on a jury is careless in considering the evidence and when a judge knowingly passes an unjust sentence.
Proverbs 17:15 — *Acquitting the guilty and condemning the innocent — the Lord detests them both.*

93. **How may you give a false testimony in your daily life?**

1. I give a false testimony when I lie about my neighbor and speak evil or carelessly gossip about anyone.

2. I give a false testimony when I use God's gift of language in a way that leads my neighbor to misunderstand what is true.
Ephesians 4:25 — *Therefore each of you must put off falsehood and speak truthfully to his neighbor, for we are all members of one body.*
James 4:11a — *Brothers, do not slander one another.*
Ephesians 4:29-32 —*Do not use harmful words, but only helpful words, the kind that build up and provide what is needed, so that what you say will do good to those who hear you. And do not make God's Holy Spirit sad; for the Spirit is God's mark of ownership on you, a guarantee that the Day will come when God will set you free. Get rid of all bitterness, passion, and anger. No more shouting and insults, no more hateful feelings of any sort. Instead, be kind and tender-hearted to one another, and forgive one another, as God has forgiven you through Christ (Today's English Version).*

94. Is it possible for you to lie by your silence?

Yes, it is possible to lie by my silence when it will lead to a misunderstanding.

95. Is it wrong for you to speak truthfully about your neighbor's faults?

1. It is wrong when I do so with an unloving heart, either because I wish to hurt my neighbor or because I am thoughtless.
Matthew 12:36 — *". . . But I tell you that men will have to give account on the day of judgment for every careless word they have spoken."*
I Corinthians 13:4-7 —*Love is patient, love is kind. It does not envy, it does not boast, it is not proud. It is not rude, it is not self-seeking, it is not easily angered, it keeps no record of wrongs. Love does not delight in evil but rejoices with the truth. It always protects, always trusts, always hopes, always perseveres.*

2. It is right when I do so because I am concerned about truth and the welfare of my neighbor.
Matthew 18:15 — *If your brother sins against you, go and show him his fault, just between the two of you. If he listens to you, you have won your brother over.*
Galatians 6:1a — *Brothers, if someone is caught in a sin, you who are spiritual should restore him gently.*

96. What does God require of you in the Eighth Commandment?

God requires that I should always be truthful and as far as the truth will permit, excuse and speak well of my neighbor.

The Ninth Commandment

You shall not covet your neighbor's house (Exodus 20:17a).

What does this mean?

This means that we should fear and love God so that we do not seek by scheming to gain possession of our neighbor's inheritance or house nor pretend to have a legal right to them but always help him to keep what is rightfully his.

97.   Why has God given the Ninth Commandment?

God has given this commandment to safeguard the place He has given us to live and to recognize the deep need people have for a place of rest and safety.

98.   What does God forbid you to do in the Ninth Commandment?

God forbids me sinfully to desire my neighbor's house.
Luke 12:15 — ..."Watch out! Be on your guard against all kinds of greed; a man's life does not consist in the abundance of his possessions."
Micah 2:1-2 — Woe to those who plan iniquity, to those who plot evil on their beds! At morning's light they carry it out because it is in their power to do it. They covet fields and seize them, and houses, and take them. They defraud a man of his home, a fellowman of his inheritance.

99.   Why is covetousness such a serious sin?

Covetousness is a serious sin because of what results from it and because it shows a lack of trust in God to give me what I need.

James 1:14,15 — ...*Each one is tempted when, by his own evil desire, he is dragged away and enticed. Then, after desire has conceived, it gives birth to sin; and sin, when it is full-grown gives birth to death.*

Galatians 5:19-21 — *The acts of the sinful nature are obvious: sexual immorality, impurity and debauchery; idolatry and witch-craft; hatred, discord, jealousy, fits of rage, selfish ambition, dissensions, factions and envy; drunkenness, orgies, and the like. I warn you, as I did before, that those who live like this will not inherit the kingdom of God.*

100. What does God require of you in the Ninth Commandment?

God requires me to help my neighbor to find and keep a place to live, and to be content with what I have.

Romans 12:13 — *Share with God's people who are in need. Practice hospitality.*

Isaiah 58:6,7 — *Is not this the kind of fasting I have chosen ... to share your food with the hungry and to provide the poor wanderer with shelter...*

I Timothy 6:6 — *Godliness with contentment is great gain.*

101. Of what should your earthly home remind you?

It should remind me that my earthly home is temporary and that God has prepared an eternal home for me. It can also remind me that God loves beauty and order and therefore my home should reflect God's love of beauty as seen in Scripture and nature.

John 14:2 — *In my Father's house are many rooms; if it were not so, I would have told you. I am going there to prepare a place for you.*

I Peter 1:3-5 — *Praise be to the God and Father of our Lord Jesus Christ! In his great mercy he has given us new birth into a living hope through the resurrection of Jesus Christ from the dead, and into an inheritance that can never perish, spoil or fade — kept in heaven for you, who through faith are shielded by God's power until the coming of the salvation that is ready to be revealed in the last time.*

102. What kinds of possessions are there?

There are useful ones and beautiful ones, both of which reflect the kind of God I have.

I Timothy 6:17 — ...*God...richly provides us with everything for our enjoyment.*

103. How should I think about my possessions?

I should realize that my possessions belong to God and that I am a caretaker of them.
Psalm 50:10-12 — ...*Every animal of the forest is mine, and the cattle on a thousand hills. I know every bird in the mountains, and the creatures of the field are mine. If I were hungry I would not tell you, for the world is mine, and all that is in it.*

The Tenth Commandment

You shall not covet your neighbor's wife, or his manservant or maidservant, his ox or donkey, or anything that belongs to your neighbor (Exodus 20:17b).

What does this mean?

This means that we should fear and love God so that we do not tempt away our neighbor's spouse or workers nor deprive him of anything that is his but encourage his wife and workers to remain loyal to him and seek to have his property stay in his possession.

104. Why has God given this commandment?

God has given this commandment to protect a person's means of making a living and forbids me to do anything which would interfere with my neighbor's ability to make a living.

105. What does God require of you in the Tenth Commandment?

God requires that I sincerely wish my neighbors all good, rejoice in their success, and help them to keep what they own.
Hebrews 13:16 — ...*Do not forget to do good and to share with others, for with such sacrifices God is pleased.*

106. How does Jesus look upon what you do for others?

Jesus looks upon what I do for others as something that I do for Him.
Matthew 25:40 — ...*"I tell you the truth, whatever you did for one of the least of these brothers of mine, you did for me."*

107. How should you guard against covetousness?

I should guard against covetousness by asking God to make me content with what I have, by wishing my neighbors every blessing, and by helping them to keep what is theirs.
I Timothy 6:6 — . . . *Godliness with contentment is great gain.*
Hebrews 13:5 — *Keep your lives free from the love of money and be content with what you have, because God has said, "Never will I leave you; never will I forsake you."*

Conclusion of the Ten Commandments

What does God say of all His commandments?

I, the Lord your God, am a jealous God, punishing the children for the sin of the fathers to the third and fourth generation of those who hate me, but showing love to a thousand generations of those who love me and keep my commandments (Exodus 20:5,6).

What does this mean?

This means that God threatens to punish all who fail to keep these commandments. We should, therefore, fear His wrath, and in no manner disobey them. But He promises grace and every blessing to all who keep them. We should, therefore, love Him, trust in Him, and gladly keep His commandments.

108.Why has God spoken these words?

God has spoken these words in order to show me that He is a holy and just God and to encourage me to keep His law and not sin against Him.
Isaiah 42:21 — *It pleased the Lord for the sake of his righteousness to make his law great and glorious.*
Isaiah 66:2 — *...This is the one I esteem; he who is humble and contrite in spirit, and trembles at my word.*
Psalm 19:7 — *The law of the Lord is perfect, reviving the soul. The statutes of the Lord are trustworthy, making wise the simple.*
I Timothy 1:8 — *We know that the law is good if one uses it properly.*

109. What does God mean when He says, "I . . . am a jealous God"?

God means that He will not share first place in the hearts and minds of His people with anyone or anything.

110. Are believing children affected by the sin of their parents?

Yes, the effects of sin are far reaching and long lasting, but so is God's love.

Lamentations 5:7 — *Our fathers sinned and are no more, and we bear their punishment.*

Lamentations 3:22 — *Because of the Lord's great love we are not consumed, for his compassions never fail.*

111. What is sin?

Sin is everything that is contrary to God's holy law and includes both inherited and actual sin.

I John 3:4 — *Everyone who sins breaks the law; in fact, sin is lawlessness.*

112. What is inherited sin (often called original sin)?

Inherited sin is the inborn tendency to wickedness, deep corruption, and evil inclination of my human nature, with no power to believe in God or save myself by my good works.

Psalm 51:5 — *Surely I was sinful at birth, sinful from the time my mother conceived me.*

Romans 5:12 —*...As sin entered the world through one man, and death through sin, ... death came to all men, because all sinned...*

113. What is actual sin?

Actual sin is all evil thoughts and desires, words, and deeds which come from inherited sin.

114. Is neglecting to do what is good as sinful as doing evil?

Yes. "Anyone ... who knows the good he ought to do and doesn't do it, sins" (James 4:17).

115. What should be your attitude toward sin?

I should hate and resist it, be deeply grieved by it, ask God's forgiveness for it, and earnestly try to put it away.

I John 2:1,2 — *My dear children, I write this to you so that you will not sin. But if anybody does sin, we have one who speaks to the Father in our defense — Jesus Christ, the Righteous One. He is the atoning sacrifice for our sins, and not only for ours but also for the sins of the whole world.*

116. Can you perfectly keep God's Ten Commandments?

No, because I was born a sinner, I cannot perfectly keep God's law.

James 2:10 — *...Whoever keeps the whole law and yet stumbles at just one point is guilty of breaking all of it.*

117. What judgment does God pronounce upon you because of your failure to obey His law perfectly?

My judgment is eternal death.

Galatians 3:10 — *All who rely on observing the law are under a curse, for it is written: "Cursed is everyone who does not continue to do everything written in the Book of the Law."*

118. What help, then, is there for you?

I may be saved through the grace of Jesus Christ offered to me in the Gospel.

John 3:16,17 — *For God so loved the world that he gave his one and only Son, that whoever believes in him shall not perish but have eternal life. For God did not send his Son into the world to condemn the world, but to save the world through him.*

119. Who alone has fulfilled the Ten Commandments for you?

Jesus alone has fulfilled the law for me by His perfect obedience.

Romans 5:10 — *For if, when we were God's enemies, we were reconciled to him through the death of his Son, how much more, having been reconciled, shall we be saved through his life!*

Prayer → 48

The Three Articles of the Creed

120. What is a creed?

A creed is a statement of belief.

121. Name the three creeds believed worldwide by Christians.

The three creeds are the Apostles' Creed, the Nicene Creed, and the Athanasian Creed.

122. Why is the creed in our catechism called the Apostles' Creed?

The creed in our catechism is called the Apostles' Creed because it is a summary statement of the Apostles' doctrine as found in the Bible.

123. When you confess the Apostles' Creed, what are you confessing?

I am confessing that I believe in one God who reveals Himself in three distinct persons; Father, Son, and Holy Spirit. This God has made all things, and continues to care for and seek to save what He has made.

124. Why do we say "I Believe" and not "We Believe" in each of the three articles of the Apostles' Creed?

We say "I Believe" because faith is personal; no one can be saved by someone else's faith.
Mark 16:16 — *Whoever believes and is baptized will be saved, but whoever does not believe will be condemned.*

125. How does God make Himself known to you?

God has made Himself known to me:

1. In the way He created, cares for, and rules the world.
Psalm 19:1 — *The heavens declare the glory of God; the skies proclaim the work of his hands.*

Romans 1:20 — *For since the creation of the world God's invisible qualities — his eternal power and divine nature — have been clearly seen, being understood from what has been made, so that men are without excuse.*

2. In my conscience, which is troubled when I do wrong and happy when I do what is right.
Romans 2:14,15 — *...They [the Gentiles] never had God's written laws, for down in their hearts they know right from wrong. God's laws are written within them; their own conscience accuses them, or sometimes excuses them (The Living Bible).*

3. In the written word, the Bible.
John 20:30,31 — *Jesus did many other miraculous signs in the presence of his disciples, which are not recorded in this book. But these are written that you may believe that Jesus is the Christ, the Son of God, and that by believing you may have life in his name.*
John 16:13 — *"But when he, the Spirit of truth, comes, he will guide you into all truth..."*

126. Who is God?

God is God. He is an eternal spirit who is loving, all-powerful, all-knowing, everywhere present, wise, good, merciful, holy, true, and just. Although God has revealed Himself to us in various ways, no human mind can fully understand Him.

God is God: Exodus 3:14 — *God said to Moses, "I am who I am. This is what you are to say to the Israelites: I AM has sent me to you."*

God is a spirit: John 4:24 — *"...God is spirit, and his worshipers must worship in spirit and in truth."*

God is eternal: Psalm 90:2 — *Before the mountains were born or you brought forth the earth and the world, from everlasting to everlasting you are God.*

God is loving: I John 4:16 — *God is love.*

God is all-powerful: Luke 1:37 — *"For nothing is impossible with God."*

God is all-knowing: I John 3:20b — *God is greater than our hearts, and he knows everything.*

God is everywhere present: Acts 17:27 — *God did this so that men would seek him and perhaps reach out for him and find him, though he is not far from each one of us.*

God is wise: Job 12:13 — *"To God belong wisdom and power; counsel and understanding are his..."*

God is good: Psalm 106:1 — *Praise the Lord. Give thanks to the Lord, for he is good; his love endures forever.*

God is merciful: Nehemiah 9:17,31 — *They [Israel] refused to listen and failed to remember the miracles you performed among them ... But in your great mercy you did not put an end to them or abandon them, for you are a gracious and merciful God.*

God is holy: Isaiah 6:3 — *"Holy, holy, holy is the Lord Almighty; the whole earth is full of his glory."*

God is true: Numbers 23:19 — *God is not a man, that he should lie, nor a son of man, that he should change his mind. Does he speak and then not act? Does he promise and not fulfill?*

God is just: Psalm 145:17 — *The Lord is righteous in all his ways and loving toward all he has made.*

127. Why is God called by Christians, God the Father, God the Son, and God the Holy Spirit?

Christians call Him God the Father, God the Son, and God the Holy Spirit because He is One Being who has shown Himself to be three persons who are equal.

128. Is there more than one God?

No, there is only one God. All other gods are imaginations of the human mind.
Deuteronomy 6:4 — *Hear, O Israel: The Lord our God, the Lord is one.*

Galatians 4:8 — *Formerly, when you did not know God, you were slaves to those who by nature are not gods.*

129. Is God the Father, older or more important than God the Son, or God the Holy Spirit?

No, the Three are One, perfectly equal in all things and have always existed.

130. Why is the teaching of the Trinity (the teaching that God is God the Father, God the Son, and God the Holy Spirit) so important?

The teaching of the Trinity is so important because it makes known the One True God in whom alone there is salvation.
John 17:3 — *Now this is eternal life: that they may know you, the only true God, and Jesus Christ whom you have sent.*

131. What is important to understand about God?

It is important to understand that everything in the universe comes under God's authority.

The First Article
Creation

I believe in God, the Father Almighty, Maker of heaven and earth.

What does this mean?

I believe that God has created me and all that exists. He has given to me and still sustains my body and soul, my senses and all my members, my reason and all the powers of my soul. I believe that He gives me food and clothing, home and family, and all material blessings; that He daily provides abundantly for all the needs of my life, protects me from all danger, and guards and keeps me from all evil. I believe that He does this because of His fatherly and divine goodness and mercy, without any merit or worthiness in me. For all this I should thank, praise, serve, and obey Him. This is most certainly true.

132. What do you mean when you say, "I believe in God, the Father"?

When I say, "I believe in God the Father," I mean that I am assured in my heart that God, who is the Father of Jesus Christ, is also my true Father, who has created me and whom I can trust in every way.
Ephesians 3:14,15 — *For this reason I kneel before the Father, from whom his whole family in heaven and on earth derives its name.*

133. **Why do you call God, the "Almighty, Maker of heaven and earth"?**

We call God the "Almighty, Maker of heaven and earth" because God is all-powerful, and by His Word He made heaven and earth and all that exists.

Genesis 1:1 — *In the beginning God created the heavens and the earth.*

Hebrews 11:3 — *By faith we understand that the universe was formed at God's command, so that what is seen was not made out of what was visible.*

134. **What does it mean to create?**

To create means to make something out of nothing.

135. **According to the Scriptures, how many kinds of created beings did God make?**

He made two kinds, invisible and visible.

136. **Who are the main invisible beings God created?**

The main invisible beings created by God are angels.

137. **Who are the angels?**

The angels are spirit beings of great number and power who were created to praise God, do His will, and serve His creation.

Psalm 103:20 — *Praise the Lord, you his angels, you mighty ones who do his bidding, who obey his word.*

Luke 2:13,14 — *Suddenly a great company of the heavenly host appeared with the angel, praising God and saying, "Glory to God in the highest, and on earth peace to men on whom his favor rests."*

Hebrews 1:14 — *Are not all angels ministering spirits sent to serve those who will inherit salvation?*

138. **Are there evil angels?**

Yes, there are evil angels who through pride and disobedience rebelled, along with Satan, against God and rejected God's will for them. They oppose God and seek to harm His creation. They are forever excluded from fellowship with Him.

II Peter 2:4 — *...God did not spare angels when they sinned, but sent them to hell, putting them into gloomy dungeons to be held for judgment...*

Ephesians 6:10-12 — *Finally, be strong in the Lord and in his mighty power. Put on the full armor of God so that you can take your stand against the devil's schemes. For our struggle is not against flesh and blood, but against the rulers, against the authorities, against the powers of this dark world and against the spiritual forces of evil in the heavenly realms.*

139. Who is Satan?

He is the main evil angel who tempted Adam and Eve in the Garden of Eden and who continues to oppose God and work against God's children.

I Peter 5:8 — *Be self-controlled and alert. Your enemy the devil prowls around like a roaring lion looking for someone to devour.*

II Corinthians 11:14 — *...Satan...masquerades as an angel of light.*

140. What are the visible beings?

People and animals are visible beings that God has created.

141. What is unique about the creation of people?

They were created in the image of God. Since God is a Spirit, this image is not a physical image.

142. According to the Scriptures, what were people like when first created by God?

1. They knew God as Creator and Friend.
2. They loved God and wanted to please Him in everything.
3. They had a conscience full of peace and joy because it was free of guilt.
4. They ruled over creation.
5. They were immune to sorrow, sickness, and death.
6. They had the ability to reason, to be creative, and to relate in love to other beings.

143. What happened to ruin this creation?

Satan deceived our first parents by tempting them to disobey God. Because they disobeyed God, sin and death spread to all other human beings.

Romans 5:12 — *Therefore, just as through one man sin entered into the world, and death through sin, and so death spread to all men, because all sinned . . . (New American Standard Version).*

144. How did our first parents sin?

They did not believe what God said, which led them to think of themselves first. They disobeyed God and tried to hide from Him. This is how the Fall happened.

145. What is meant by the Fall?

The Fall refers to Adam and Eve's unbelief and disobedience in the Garden of Eden which brought terrible results to themselves and to all creation.

146. What is the natural condition of people since the Fall?

1. Since the Fall, people are unable truly to know God and understand what He does.

II Corinthians 4:4 — *The god of this age has blinded the minds of unbelievers, so that they cannot see the light of the gospel of the glory of Christ, who is the image of God.*

I Corinthians 2:14 — *The man without the Spirit does not accept the things that come from the Spirit of God, for they are foolishness to him, and he cannot understand them, because they are spiritually discerned.*

2. Since the Fall, people are unable to love God or please Him, and instead are slaves to evil desires.

Romans 8:7,8 — *...The sinful mind is hostile to God. It does not submit to God's law, nor can it do so. Those controlled by the sinful nature cannot please God.*

3. Since the Fall, the conscience is bothered because of guilt.

Genesis 3:8-10 — *Then the man and his wife heard the sound of the Lord God as he was walking in the garden in the cool of the day, and they hid from the Lord God among the trees of the garden. But the Lord God called to the man, "Where are you?" He answered, "I heard you in the garden, and I was afraid because I was naked; so I hid."*

4. Since the Fall, people suffer because of sorrow, sickness, and death.
Job 14:1 — *"Man born of woman is of few days and full of trouble. He springs up like a flower and withers away; like a fleeting shadow, he does not endure."*

5. Since the Fall, people no longer rule creation as they once did.
Genesis 3:17b-19 — *"Cursed is the ground because of you; through painful toil you will eat of it all the days of your life. It will produce thorns and thistles for you, and you will eat the plants of the field. By the sweat of your brow you will eat your food until you return to the ground, since from it you were taken; for dust you are and to dust you will return."*

147. How has the rest of God's creation been affected by the Fall?

Everything decays or grows old and dies.
Romans 8:22 — *We know that the whole creation has been groaning as in the pains of childbirth right up to the present time.*

148. How should you think about the rest of creation?

I should remind myself of God's greatness, and care for, and wisely use His creation.
Psalm 8:1-9 — *O Lord, our Lord, how majestic is your name in all the earth! You have set your glory above the heavens. From the lips of children and infants you have ordained praise because of your enemies, to silence the foe and the avenger. When I consider your heavens, the work of your fingers, the moon and the stars, which you have set in place, what is man that you are mindful of him, the son of man that you care for him? You made him a little lower than the heavenly beings and crowned him with glory and honor. You made him ruler over the works of your hands; you put everything under his feet: all flocks and herds,*

*and the beasts of the field, the birds of the air, and the fish of the
sea, all that swim the paths of the seas. O Lord, our Lord, how
majestic is your name in all the earth!*

149. Did God forsake His creation because of the Fall?

No, Adam and Eve and their descendants deserved to be forsaken,
but God promised and sent them a Savior. He continues to
preserve and rule all things which otherwise would disintegrate.
Genesis 3:15 — *"And I will put enmity between you and the
woman, and between your offspring and hers; he will crush your
head, and you will strike his heel."*
Genesis 8:21b-22 — *"Never again will I curse the ground because of man, even though every inclination of his heart is evil
from childhood. And never again will I destroy all living creatures, as I have done. As long as the earth endures, seedtime and
harvest, cold and heat, summer and winter, day and night will
never cease."*
Hebrews 1:3a — *The Son is the radiance of God's glory and the
exact representation of his being, sustaining all things by his
powerful word.*

150. Did God ever repeat His promise to send a Savior?

Yes, He repeated His promise to Abraham, Isaac, and Jacob, and
to Moses and the Prophets.

151. When was Christ sent into the world?

Christ came at the time in history chosen and prepared by God
Himself.
Galatians 4:4,5 — *...When the time had fully come, God sent his
Son, born of a woman, born under law, to redeem those under
law, that we might receive the full rights of sons.*
John 3:16 — *For God so loved the world that he gave his one and
only Son, that whoever believes in him shall not perish but have
eternal life.*

152. How does God preserve you and all His other creatures?

God cares for me and all His other creatures as a loving Father.

Psalm 145:15,16 — *The eyes of all look to you and you give them their food at the proper time. You open your hand and satisfy the desires of every living thing.*

Matthew 5:45b — *He causes his sun to rise on the evil and good, and sends rain on the righteous and the unrighteous.*

153. How does God control all things?

God directs all things according to His wise and perfect will. Although God's ways are not always clear to me, I am told in the Bible that they are always the best.

Romans 8:28 — *...We know that in all things God works for the good of those who love him, who have been called according to his purpose.*

Isaiah 55:8,9 — *"For my thoughts are not your thoughts, neither are your ways my ways," declares the Lord. "As the heavens are higher than the earth, so are my ways higher than your ways and my thoughts than your thoughts."*

Jeremiah 29:11 — *"For I know the plans I have for you," declares the Lord, "plans to prosper you and not to harm you, plans to give you hope and a future."*

Psalm 91:11 — *For he will command his angels concerning you to guard you in all your ways.*

154. What do you and all other human beings deserve because of the Fall?

I deserve God's wrath and condemnation.

Ezekiel 18:4b — *The soul who sins is the one who will die.*

Romans 5:18a — *...The result of one trespass was condemnation for all men...*

155. What then has God done for you?

God has in love sent His one and only son, Jesus Christ, to be my Savior, to save me from my sin and God's wrath and condemnation.

John 3:17 — *For God did not send his Son into the world to condemn the world, but to save the world through him.*

Ephesians 1:4 — *...He chose us in him before the creation of the world to be holy and blameless in his sight.*

II Timothy 1:9 — *[God] has saved us and called us to a holy life — not because of anything we have done but because of his own purpose and grace. This grace was given us in Christ Jesus before the beginning of time...*

156. **What is God's purpose for you and the world?**

God's purpose is to recreate His image in me and to make a new heaven and a new earth.

The Second Article
Redemption

I believe in Jesus Christ, His only Son, our Lord, who was conceived by the Holy Spirit, born of the Virgin Mary, suffered under Pontius Pilate, was crucified, dead, and buried; He descended into hell; the third day He rose again from the dead; He ascended into heaven, and is seated at the right hand of God the Father Almighty, from whence He shall come to judge the living and the dead.

What does this mean?

I believe that Jesus Christ, true God, begotten of the Father from eternity, and also true man, born of the Virgin Mary, is my Lord, who has redeemed me, a lost and condemned creature, bought and freed me from all sins, from death, and from the power of the devil — not with silver and gold, but with His holy and precious blood, and with His innocent sufferings and death — in order that I might be His own, live under Him in His Kingdom, and serve Him in everlasting righteousness, innocence, and blessedness; even as He is risen from the dead, and lives and reigns to all eternity. This is most certainly true.

157. What do you mean when you say, "I believe in Jesus Christ"?

When I say I believe in Jesus Christ, I mean that I am assured by God in my heart that Jesus Christ alone is my Savior. In Him I have eternal life and He is my Lord to whom I owe allegiance.
John 17:3 — *Now this is eternal life: that they may know you, the only true God, and Jesus Christ, whom you have sent.*
Acts 4:12 — *Salvation is found in no one else, for there is no other name under heaven given to men by which we must be saved.*
John 3:36 — *Whoever believes in the Son has eternal life, but whoever rejects the Son will not see life, for God's wrath remains on him.*

158. What is the main teaching of the Second Article?

The Second Article teaches me about Jesus Christ and all His sufferings to save me from the guilt of sin, from death, and from the power of the devil.

159. Who is Jesus Christ?

Jesus Christ is true God, begotten of the Father, and therefore without beginning, and true man, born of the Virgin Mary.
John 1:1,14 — *In the beginning was the Word, and the Word was with God, and the Word was God ... The Word became flesh and made his dwelling among us. We have seen his glory, the glory of the One and Only, who came from the Father, full of grace and truth.*
Matthew 1:21 — *She [Mary] will give birth to a son, and you are to give him the name Jesus, because he will save his people from their sins.*

160. Does Jesus then have both a human and a divine nature?

Yes, Jesus has a divine nature from God, the Father from eternity; the human nature He took on Himself from His mother, Mary.
Matthew 1:18-23 — *This is how the birth of Jesus Christ came about: His mother Mary was pledged to be married to Joseph, but before they came together, she was found to be with child through the Holy Spirit. Because Joseph her husband was a*

righteous man and did not want to expose her to public disgrace, he had in mind to divorce her quietly.

But after he had considered this, an angel of the Lord appeared to him in a dream and said, "Joseph, son of David, do not be afraid to take Mary home as your wife, because what is conceived in her is from the Holy Spirit. She will give birth to a son, and you are to give him the name Jesus, because he will save his people from their sins."

All this took place to fulfill what the Lord had said through the prophet: "The virgin will be with child and will give birth to a son, and they will call him Immanuel" — which means, "God with us."

Colossians 2:9 — *For in Christ all the fullness of the Deity lives in bodily form...*

161. How does the Bible show that Jesus Christ is true God?

The Bible shows that Jesus Christ is true God by what it teaches about Him and what it says He did (For example: compare John 1:1-3 with Ephesians 3:9 and Colossians 1:16; compare Hebrews 1:1-6 with Matthew 4:10 and Deuteronomy 6:13 — note who alone is to be worshiped; the *I am's* of the Gospel according to John, 6:35, 8:12, 10:11, 11:25, 14:6, and 15:1, all show that Jesus is true God; Jesus' own resurrection recorded in all the Gospels, Matthew 28:1-10, Mark 16:1-8, Luke 24:1-11, and John 20:1-18, show that He is God — see Thomas' testimony in John 20:28; see also Matthew 28:20, John 21:17, John 5:23, Revelation 22:13, Isaiah 9:6, Matthew 8:27, Titus 2:13, and I John 5:20).

162. Why was it necessary for our Savior to be true man?

It was necessary for our Savior to be true man in order that He might fulfill the law for us, and suffer and die in our place.

Galatians 4:4,5 — *...When the time had fully come, God sent his Son, born of a woman, born under law, to redeem those under law, that we might receive the full rights of sons.*

Romans 5:19 — *For just as through the disobedience of the one man the many were made sinners, so also through the obedience of the one man the many will be made righteous.*

I Timothy 2:5-6 — *For there is one God and one mediator between God and men, the man Christ Jesus, who gave himself as a ransom for all men...*

163. Why was it necessary for our Savior to be true God?

It was necessary for our Savior to be true God so that His blood might have unlimited power to pay for the sins of all people.
Hebrews 9:12 — *He did not enter by means of the blood of goats and calves; but he entered the Most Holy Place once for all by his own blood, having obtained eternal redemption.*

164. What does the Bible teach about the birth of Jesus?

The Bible teaches that Jesus was conceived by the Holy Spirit and was therefore without sin. It also teaches that He was born at Bethlehem in great poverty and lowliness.
Luke 1:35 — *The angel answered, "The Holy Spirit will come upon you, and the power of the Most High will overshadow you. So the holy one to be born will be called the Son of God.*
Luke 2:7 — *And she gave birth to her firstborn, a son. She wrapped him in cloths and placed him in a manger, because there was no room for them in the inn.*
Matthew 8:20 — *Jesus replied, "Foxes have holes and birds of the air have nests, but the Son of Man has no place to lay his head."*

165. What word do we use to describe the coming of God into the world in the person of Jesus?

The word we use to describe this is *incarnation,* which means *in flesh.*
John 1:14 — *The Word became flesh and made his dwelling among us. We have seen his glory, the glory of the One and Only, who came from the Father, full of grace and truth.*
Philippians 2:6,7 — *[Jesus Christ] Who, being in very nature God, did not consider equality with God something to be grasped, but made himself nothing, taking the very nature of a servant, being made in human likeness.*

166. What does the name Jesus mean?

The name *Jesus* means *Savior.*
Matthew 1:21 — *She will give birth to a son, and you are to give him the name Jesus, because he will save his people from their sins.*

167. What does the word Christ mean when given as a title for Jesus?

The title *Christ* means *Anointed One* or *one set apart by God to be the Savior.*

168. How was Jesus anointed?

God anointed Jesus with the Holy Spirit and with power.
Acts 10:38 — *"...God anointed Jesus of Nazareth with the Holy Spirit and power, and...he went around doing good and healing all who were under the power of the devil, because God was with him."*

169. What was Jesus sent to be for you?

He was sent to be my Prophet, High Priest, and King.

170. What does it mean to you that Jesus was sent to be the Prophet?

As Prophet, Jesus came to show me what God is like and to show me the way of salvation.
Acts 3:22 — *For Moses said, "The Lord your God will raise up for you a prophet like me from among your own people; you must listen to everything he tells you."*

171. What does it mean to you that Jesus was sent to be the High Priest?

As High Priest, Jesus offered up himself as a sacrifice for my sins, and represents me in the presence of the Father and continually prays for me.

Hebrews 7:27 — *Unlike the other high priests, he [Jesus] does not need to offer sacrifices day after day, first for his own sins, and then for the sins of the people. He sacrificed for their sins once for all when he offered himself.*

Romans 8:33,34 — *Who would dare to accuse us, whom God has chosen? The judge himself has declared us free from sin. Who is in a position to condemn? Only Christ, and Christ died for us, Christ rose for us, Christ reigns in power for us, Christ prays for us! (The New Testament in Modern English* by J.B. Phillips).

172. What does it mean to you that Jesus was sent to be King?

As King, Jesus rules a kingdom that goes beyond the boundaries of this earth. He defends all its members against its enemies. He will rule this kingdom forever.

Isaiah 9:6,7 — *For to us a child is born, to us a son is given and the government will be on his shoulders. And he will be called Wonderful Counselor, Mighty God, Everlasting Father, Prince of Peace. Of the increase of his government and peace there will be no end. He will reign on David's throne and over his kingdom, establishing and upholding it with justice and righteousness from that time on and forever. The zeal of the Lord Almighty will accomplish this.*

173. Why is Jesus Christ called Savior?

Jesus Christ is called Savior because He has redeemed me, a lost and condemned sinner.

174. How has Christ redeemed you?

Christ has redeemed me by paying for my sins with His holy and precious blood, and with His innocent sufferings and death; and by fulfilling the law in my place by His perfect life and complete obedience.

I Peter 1:18,19 — *For you know that it was not with perishable things such as silver or gold that you were redeemed from the empty way of life handed down to you from your forefathers, but with the precious blood of Christ, a lamb without blemish or defect.*

175. What does the word redeem mean?

The word *redeem* means *to buy back* or *to set someone free by paying a ransom.*

176. Who were the ones Jesus Christ redeemed?

He has redeemed all people, including me, a lost and condemned sinner.
I John 2:2 — *He [Jesus] is the atoning sacrifice for our sins, and not only for ours but also for the sins of the whole world.*

177. Even though you are redeemed in this way, may you be eternally lost?

Yes, I may be eternally lost if I reject, neglect, or ignore Christ's redemption.
John 3:18 — *Whoever believes in him [Jesus] is not condemned, but whoever does not believe stands condemned already because he has not believed in the name of God's one and only Son.*
Hebrews 2:1,3 — *We must pay more careful attention, therefore, to what we have heard, so that we do not drift away ... How shall we escape if we ignore such a great salvation?*

178. How are you saved?

I am saved by God's gift of faith to me. This saving faith was first given to me when I was baptized and continues to be given to me by God's Spirit through the Word as I repent of my sin and trust Jesus alone for my salvation.
Acts 2:21 — *...Everyone who calls on the name of the Lord will be saved.*
Acts 16:31 — *They [Paul and Silas] replied [to the Philippian jailer], "Believe in the Lord Jesus, and you will be saved — you and your household."*

179. What blessings come to you because you are redeemed by Christ?

Jesus Christ has bought and freed me from the power of sin, death, and Satan, and has made me an heir of eternal life.

Colossians 1:13,14 — *For he [God] has rescued us from the dominion of darkness and brought us into the kingdom of the Son he loves, in whom we have redemption, the forgiveness of sins.*

180. What did Christ do when He redeemed you from sin?

1. He took on Himself my guilt and the punishment for my sin.
Galatians 3:13a — *Christ redeemed us from the curse of the law by becoming a curse for us.*

2. He broke the power of sin so it no longer should dominate my life.
Romans 6:14 — *For sin shall not be your master, because you are not under law, but under grace.*

3. He promised that someday I will be free from the presence of sin.
I John 3:2b — *...We know that when he [Jesus] appears, we shall be like him, for we shall see him as he is.*

181. How does being redeemed by Christ make you free from death?

1. Physical death will become an entrance for me into the place Jesus has prepared for all believers.
John 14:1,2 — *"Do not let your hearts be troubled. Trust in God; trust also in me. In my Father's house are many rooms; if it were not so, I would have told you. I am going there to prepare a place for you."*

2. Spiritual death has lost its power over me.
John 5:24 — *"I tell you the truth, whoever hears my word and believes him who sent me has eternal life and will not be condemned; he has crossed over from death to life."*

3. Eternal death in hell will not touch me.
Romans 6:23 — *For the wages of sin is death, but the gift of God is eternal life in Christ Jesus our Lord.*

182. Does being redeemed by Christ free you from the power of Satan?

Yes, when Jesus died and rose again, He showed that Satan was defeated. Each day, I can by faith claim the victory of Christ over Satan in my daily life.

I John 3:8b — *The reason the Son of God appeared was to destroy the devil's work.*

Colossians 2:15 — *...Having disarmed the powers and authorities, he [Jesus] made a public spectacle of them, triumphing over them by the cross.*

I Peter 5:8,9 — *Be self-controlled and alert. Your enemy the devil prowls around like a roaring lion looking for someone to devour. Resist him, standing firm in the faith, because you know that your brothers throughout the world are undergoing the same kind of sufferings.*

183. Why has Christ redeemed you?

Christ has redeemed me in order that I might belong to Him, be a citizen in His Kingdom, and serve Him perfectly and happily without guilt, forever.

II Corinthians 5:15 — *[Jesus]...died for all, that those who live should no longer live for themselves but for him who died for them and was raised again.*

Luke 1:69,74,75 — *He has raised up a horn of salvation for us in the house of his servant David...to rescue us from the hand of our enemies, and to enable us to serve him without fear in holiness and righteousness before him all our days.*

184. How did Christ become Savior and Redeemer of the world?

Christ became Savior and Redeemer of the world by humbling Himself and by becoming obedient to death, even death on a cross (Philippians 2:8).

185. What are five stages in the humiliation of Christ?

Five stages in the humiliation of Christ are: 1) His birth in poverty; 2) His suffering under Pontius Pilate; 3) His crucifixion; 4) His death; and 5) His burial.

186. Why did Christ begin His earthly life with birth in poverty?

Christ began His earthly life with birth in poverty in order to identify fully with our human condition, to sanctify our entire life, and to make us rich.

II Corinthians 8:9 — *For you know the grace of our Lord Jesus Christ, that though he was rich, yet for your sakes he became poor, so that you through his poverty might become rich.*

187. What are some of the sufferings Jesus endured?

He was betrayed into the hands of His enemies by one of His own disciples; He was bound, beaten, and whipped; He was made fun of, spit upon, crowned with thorns, and finally nailed to the cross.

188. When did Jesus' suffering become greatest?

Jesus suffered all His life, but His greatest suffering came in the Garden of Gethsemane, on the night when he was betrayed, when His sweat was like drops of blood, and on the cross when He cried in agony of soul, "My God, My God, why have you forsaken me?" (Matthew 26:36-46; Matthew 27:46; Luke 22:44).

189. What was crucifixion?

Crucifixion was a painful, disgraceful, and cursed means of execution by which criminals were fastened to a cross and allowed to die.

190. How did Jesus accept His suffering?

Jesus accepted His suffering willingly and patiently.

Philippians 2:8 — *And being found in appearance as a man, he [Jesus] humbled himself and became obedient to death — even death on a cross!*

Isaiah 53:7 — *He was oppressed and afflicted, yet he did not open his mouth; he was led like a lamb to the slaughter, and as a sheep before her shearers is silent, so he did not open his mouth.*

191. Of what benefit is the death of Jesus to you?

By His death, Jesus willingly suffered the punishment of sin as my substitute. Because of His death, I am no longer God's enemy and can have fellowship with Him.

II Corinthians 5:19,21 — *...God was reconciling the world to himself in Christ, not counting men's sins against them. God made him who had no sin to be sin for us, so that in him we might become the righteousness of God.*

192. What comfort do you find in Christ's burial?

The burial of Christ assures me that He has buried my sins, that He has gone ahead of me to the grave and taken away its power, and that when I die, He will be present with me so that I need not be afraid.

Psalm 23 — *The Lord is my shepherd, I shall not be in want. He makes me lie down in green pastures, he leads me beside quiet waters, he restores my soul. He guides me in paths of righteousness for his name's sake. Even though I walk through the valley of the shadow of death, I will fear no evil, for you are with me; your rod and your staff, they comfort me. You prepare a table before me in the presence of my enemies. You anoint my head with oil; my cup overflows. Surely goodness and love will follow me all the days of my life, and I will dwell in the house of the Lord forever.*

193. What are five stages in the exaltation of Christ?

Five stages in the exaltation of Christ are: 1) His descent into hell*; 2) His resurrection; 3) His ascension; 4) His mediation at the right hand of God the Father; 5) His second coming.

194. Why did Christ descend into hell*?

Christ descended into hell to announce the victory He had won over death and Satan (I Peter 3:18,19).

---

*   *Hell,* as used here, does not refer to the place of final punishment. It refers rather to *Hades,* a place for the spirits of the dead between death and final punishment or reward.

195. **What benefits do you have because of the resurrection of Christ?**

1. The resurrection assures me that Jesus is the Son of God.
Romans 1:4 — *[Jesus] through the Spirit of holiness was declared with power to be the Son of God by his resurrection from the dead...*

2. The resurrection assures me that Jesus has fully paid for my sins.
Romans 4:25 — *He [Jesus] was delivered over to death for our sins and was raised to life for our justification.*

3. The resurrection gives me power to arise from spiritual death, and to live a new life.
Romans 6:4 — *We were therefore buried with him through baptism into death in order that, just as Christ was raised from the dead through the glory of the Father, we too may live a new life.*

4. The resurrection assures me that I shall rise on the last day.
I Corinthians 15:20,21 — *But Christ has indeed been raised from the dead, the firstfruits of those who have fallen asleep. For since death came through a man [Adam], the resurrection of the dead comes also through a man [Jesus].*

196.How did Jesus make His resurrection known?

During a period of forty days, He showed Himself alive to many people and spoke to them about the Kingdom of God (Luke 24; John 20:10-29; John 21:1-23; I Corinthians 15:3-9).

197.What command did Jesus give His disciples before His ascension?

Jesus gave them this command: "...All authority in heaven and on earth has been given to me. Therefore go and make disciples of all nations, baptizing them in the name of the Father and of the Son and of the Holy Spirit, and teaching them to obey everything I have commanded you. And surely I am with you always, to the very end of the age" (Matthew 28:18-20).

198. What does the Bible teach about Jesus' ascension into heaven?

The Bible teaches that Jesus, as God, and also as a human being, visibly and bodily left the earth as our forerunner and took His place at the right hand of God the Father.

Acts 1:11 — *"Men of Galilee," they said, "why do you stand here looking into the sky? This same Jesus, who has been taken from you into heaven, will come back in the same way you have seen him go into heaven."*

Hebrews 9:24 — *For Christ did not enter a manmade sanctuary that was only a copy of the true one; he entered heaven itself, now to appear for us in God's presence.*

199. What does the Bible teach about Jesus sitting at the right hand of God the Father?

The Bible teaches that Jesus, as our representative, shares God's power and glory, rules all things, prays for us, and with the Father sends us the Holy Spirit.

I Peter 3:22 — *[Jesus] has gone into heaven and is at God's right hand — with angels, authorities and powers in submission to him.*

200. How is Christ still present on earth?

Christ is present on the earth invisibly but powerfully.

Matthew 28:20 — *"...Surely I am with you always, to the very end of the age."*

201. What promise did Jesus give about His visible return to this earth?

He gave this promise, "I will come back and take you to be with me that you also may be where I am" (John 14:3).

202. What does the Bible teach about Jesus' return?

The Bible teaches that:

1. Jesus will visibly return to earth.

Acts 1:11 — *"Men of Galilee," they said, "why do you stand here looking into the sky? This same Jesus, who has been taken from you into heaven, will come back in the same way you have seen him go into heaven."*

2. Jesus will raise the dead.
I Thessalonians 4:16 — *For the Lord himself will come down from heaven, with a loud command, with the voice of the archangel and with the trumpet call of God, and the dead in Christ will rise first.*

3. Jesus will judge the living and the dead according to His word.
Matthew 12:36,37 — *"...I tell you that men will have to give account on the day of judgment for every careless word they have spoken. For by your words you will be acquitted, and by your words you will be condemned."*

4. Jesus will create a new heaven and a new earth.
II Peter 3:10-13 — *But the day of the Lord will come like a thief. The heavens will disappear with a roar; the elements will be destroyed by fire, and the earth and everything in it will be laid bare. Since everything will be destroyed in this way, what kind of people ought you to be? You ought to live holy and godly lives as you look forward to the day of God and speed its coming. That day will bring about the destruction of the heavens by fire, and the elements will melt in the heat. But in keeping with His promise we are looking forward to a new heaven and a new earth, the home of righteousness.*

5. Jesus will take His children to be with Him forever.
John 14:1-4 — *"Do not let your hearts be troubled. Trust in God; trust also in me. In my Father's house are many rooms; if it were not so, I would have told you. I am going there to prepare a place for you. And if I go and prepare a place for you, I will come back and take you to be with me that you also may be where I am. You know the way to the place where I am going."*

6. Jesus will reign as king forever.
Revelation 11:15c — *"The kingdom of the world has become the kingdom of our Lord and of his Christ, and he will reign for ever and ever."*

203. When will Jesus return?

Jesus says that no one knows the exact time of His return, but He has given us certain signs which show that He may return at any time.

Matthew 24:44 — *"...So you also must be ready, because the Son of Man will come at an hour when you do not expect him..."*

Matthew 24:36 — *"No one knows about the day or hour, not even the angels in heaven, nor the Son, but only the Father...*

204. What are some signs of Jesus' return?

Signs that point to Jesus' return at any time are:

1. The preaching of the gospel (Matthew 24:14).

2. Increasing ungodliness among people (II Timothy 3:1-5).

3. Wars and rumors of war (Matthew 24:6).

4. Catastrophes in nature (Matthew 24:7).

5. False Christs will appear and deceive many (Matthew 24:4; II Thessalonians 2:3-8).

205. Is it enough for you to know all these things about Christ and consider them to be true in order to be saved?

No, the Holy Spirit must teach me to know Christ as my Savior from sin.

John 3:5-8 — *Jesus answered, "I tell you the truth, no one can enter the kingdom of God unless he is born of water and the Spirit. Flesh gives birth to flesh, but the Spirit gives birth to spirit. You should not be surprised at my saying, You must be born again. The wind blows wherever it pleases. You hear its sound, but you cannot tell where it comes from or where it is going. So it is with everyone born of the Spirit."*

I Corinthians 12:3 — *...No one can say, "Jesus is Lord," except by the Holy Spirit.*

The Third Article
Sanctification

I believe in the Holy Spirit, the holy Christian church, the communion of saints, the forgiveness of sins, the resurrection of the body, and the life everlasting. Amen.

What does this mean?

I believe that I cannot by my own reason or strength believe in Jesus Christ, my Lord, or come to Him, but the Holy Spirit has called me through the Gospel, enlightened me with His gifts, and sanctified and preserved me in the true faith, just as He calls, gathers, enlightens, and sanctifies the whole Christian church on earth, and preserves it in union with Jesus Christ in the one true faith, in which Christian church He daily forgives abundantly all my sins, and the sins of all believers, and at the last day will raise up me and all the dead, and will grant everlasting life to me and to all who believe in Christ. This is most certainly true.

206. What do you mean when you say, "I believe in the Holy Spirit"?

When I say I believe in the Holy Spirit, I mean that I place myself in the care of the Holy Spirit and trust Him to help me believe in Christ and live by God's Word.
John 14:26 — ...*The Counselor, the Holy Spirit, whom the Father will send in my name, will teach you all things and will remind you of everything I have said to you.*

207. Who is the Holy Spirit?

The Holy Spirit is the third person of the Trinity and true God with the Father and the Son.

208. What is the work of the Holy Spirit?

The work of the Holy Spirit is to call, gather, enlighten, sanctify, and preserve.

209. How does the Holy Spirit call you?

The Holy Spirit calls me to faith in Christ by the Gospel in Word and Sacraments.
Romans 10:17 — *...Faith comes from hearing the message, and the message is heard through the word of Christ.*
II Thessalonians 2:14 — *He called you to this [salvation] through our gospel, that you might share in the glory of our Lord Jesus Christ.*

210. What other ways does the Holy Spirit use to call you or to get your attention?

The Holy Spirit uses sufferings, blessings, and the example of others to get my attention.
II Corinthians 7:10 — *Godly sorrow brings repentance that leads to salvation and leaves no regret, but worldly sorrow brings death.*
Romans 2:4b — *...God's kindness leads you toward repentance...*
I Timothy 4:12 — *Don't let anyone look down on you because you are young, but set an example for the believers in speech, in life, in love, in faith, and in purity.*

211. Why might you not pay attention to the call of the Holy Spirit?

I might not pay attention to the call of the Holy Spirit because:

1. The ways of the world are so appealing to me.

2. My human nature desires the ways of the world.

3. I do not appreciate the goodness of God's ways.

4. I want to go my own way.
Isaiah 65:2 — *All day long I have held out my hands to an obstinate people, who walk in ways not good, pursuing their own imaginations...*
Isaiah 53:6a — *We all, like sheep, have gone astray, each of us has turned to his own way...*

212. Why is it dangerous not to pay attention to the call of the Holy Spirit and refuse to come to Jesus?

It is dangerous to do this because I may become hardened so that I no longer desire to come to Jesus nor care whether or not I have His salvation.
Isaiah 55:6,7 — *Seek the Lord while he may be found; call on him while he is near. Let the wicked forsake his way and the evil man his thoughts. Let him turn to the Lord, and he will have mercy on him, and to our God, for he will freely pardon.*
Hebrews 3:12,13 — *See to it...that none of you has a sinful, unbelieving heart that turns away from the living God. But encourage one another daily, as long as it is called Today, so that none of you may be hardened by sin's deceitfulness.*

213. How do you listen to the call of the Holy Spirit?

I listen to the call of the Holy Spirit by repenting and believing the Gospel of Jesus.

214. What does it mean for you to repent?

I repent when I agree and feel deeply sorry that I have not kept and cannot keep God's law, and when I receive the good news that Jesus died for me.
I John 1:8-10 — *If we claim to be without sin, we deceive ourselves and the truth is not in us. If we confess our sins, he is faithful and just and will forgive us our sins and purify us from all unrighteousness. If we claim we have not sinned, we make him out to be a liar and his word has no place in our lives.*
Proverbs 28:13 — *He who conceals his sins does not prosper, but whoever confesses and renounces them finds mercy.*

215. What does it mean that the Holy Spirit has enlightened you?

To be enlightened by the Holy Spirit means that through hearing God's Word, the Holy Spirit helps me to see my sinfulness and to believe that Jesus is my Savior.
John 16:13 — ...*When he, the Spirit of truth, comes, he will guide you into all the truth.*

216. Why do you need the enlightenment of the Holy Spirit?

I need the enlightenment of the Holy Spirit because by my own reason I am unable truly to know God or the things that He has done and said in His Word.
II Corinthians 4:4 — *The god of this age has blinded the minds of unbelievers, so that they cannot see the light of the gospel of the glory of Christ, who is the image of God.*
I Corinthians 2:14 — *The man without the Spirit does not accept the things that come from the Spirit of God, for they are foolishness to him, and he cannot understand them, because they are spiritually discerned.*

217. How can you truly know God?

I can truly know God through faith in Jesus Christ as shown to me in the Gospel.
John 17:3 — *Now this is eternal life: that they may know you, the only true God, and Jesus Christ, whom you have sent.*

218. What is a true and living faith in Jesus Christ?

When I as a repentant sinner receive Jesus Christ as my only Savior from sin, death, and the power of the devil, and find refuge in Him and confidently rely upon Him, then I have a true and living faith in Jesus Christ. Furthermore, a true and living faith will show itself by good works.
Matthew 5:16 — *"...Let your light shine before men, that they may see your good deeds and praise your Father in heaven..."*
James 2:17 — *...Faith by itself, if it is not accompanied by action, is dead.*

Ephesians 2:10 — *For we are God's workmanship, created in Christ Jesus to do good works, which God prepared in advance for us to do.*

219. Is it possible for you to receive this faith?

Yes, Jesus gives faith to all who repent.
Acts 16:30b,31 — *... "Sirs, what must I[the jailor] do to be saved?" They [Paul and Silas] replied, "Believe in the Lord Jesus, and you will be saved — you and your household."*

220. How does God show His graciousness as you turn to Him?

God shows His graciousness to me by freely accepting me as I turn to Him even though my faith may be very weak or when I hardly dare accept His grace.
Mark 9:24b — *"I do believe; help me overcome my unbelief!"*
Isaiah 42:1-3 — *"Here is my servant, whom I uphold, my chosen one in whom I delight; I will put my spirit on him and he will bring justice to the nations. He will not shout or cry out, or raise his voice in the streets. A bruised reed he will not break, and a smoldering wick he will not snuff out.*

221. What benefits come to you as you believe in Jesus?

I receive the gifts of justification, the new birth, sanctification, and one day will receive the gift of glorification.

222. What is justification?

Justification is the gracious act of God by which He, for Christ's sake, acquits me(declares me not guilty), a repentant and believing sinner of my sin and guilt, credits me with Christ's righteousness, and looks upon me, in Christ, as though I had never sinned.
Ephesians 2:8 — *For it is by grace you have been saved, through faith — and this not from yourselves, it is the gift of God...*
II Corinthians 5:21 — *God made him [Jesus] who had no sin to be sin for us, so that in him we might become the righteousness of God.*

Isaiah 53:5 — *But he was pierced for our transgressions, he was crushed for our iniquities; the punishment that brought us peace was upon him, and by his wounds we are healed.*

223. What gifts come to you because of justification?

Because of justification I have received:

1. Adoption as God's child.
Romans 8:15,17a — *For you did not receive a spirit that makes you a slave again to fear, but you received the Spirit of sonship [or adoption]...Now if we are children, then we are heirs — heirs of God and co-heirs with Christ...*

2. Peace with God.

3. Joy in suffering.

4. Hope.

5. The love of God.

6. The Holy Spirit.
Romans 5:1-5 — *Therefore, since we have been justified through faith, we have peace with God through our Lord Jesus Christ, through whom we have gained access by faith into this grace in which we now stand. And we rejoice in the hope of the glory of God. Not only so, but we also rejoice in our sufferings, because we know that suffering produces perseverance; perseverance, character; and character, hope. And hope does not disappoint us, because God has poured out his love into our hearts by the Holy Spirit, whom he has given us.*

224. Why should the church always hold and teach this doctrine of justification by grace alone?

The church must always hold and teach this doctrine because it is the chief doctrine of the Christian religion; it distinguishes the Christian religion from false religion which teaches salvation by works; it gives enduring comfort to the repentant sinner; and it gives all glory to God.

225. For whose sake does God forgive you your sins?

God does not forgive my sins because I deserve it, but only because of what Christ did on the cross, when His blood paid for the sins of the whole world.

I John 2:1,2 — *My dear children, I write this to you so that you will not sin. But if anybody does sin, we have one who speaks to the Father in our defense — Jesus Christ, the Righteous One. He is the atoning sacrifice for our sins, and not only for ours but also for the sins of the whole world.*

226. What happens to you when your sins are forgiven?

When God forgives me my sins for the sake of Jesus Christ, He blots them all out, and I do not have them any more.

Isaiah 43:25 — *"I, even I, am he who blots out your transgressions, for my own sake, and remembers your sins no more..."*

Isaiah 1:18 — *"Come now, let us reason together," says the Lord. "Though your sins are like scarlet, they shall be as white as snow; though they are red as crimson, they shall be like wool..."*

227. Why is this such good news?

This is good news because my sins stand between me and God, and without this forgiveness I would spend eternity in hell without God.

John 3:36 — *"Whoever believes in the Son has eternal life, but whoever rejects the Son will not see life, for God's wrath remains on him."*

Romans 8:1 — *Therefore, there is now no condemnation for those who are in Christ Jesus, because through Christ Jesus the law of the Spirit of life set me free from the law of sin and death.*

228. What is the new birth?

The new birth, sometimes called regeneration, is the gracious work of the Holy Spirit by which He, because He has come to live in my heart, renews the image of God in me, and creates a new spiritual being.

II Corinthians 5:17 — *Therefore, if anyone is in Christ, he is a new creation; the old has gone, the new has come!*

John 1:12,13 — ...*To all who receive him, to those who believed in his name, he gave the right to become children of God — children born not of natural descent, nor of human decision or a husband's will, but born of God.*

Ephesians 4:22-24 — *You were taught, with regard to your former way of life, to put off your old self, which is being corrupted by its deceitful desires; to be made new in the attitude of your minds; and to put on the new self, created to be like God in true righteousness and holiness.*

229. In what ways does this new birth affect you?

The Holy Spirit through the new birth changes me in the following ways:

1. He gives me a love for God.
I John 4:19 — *We love because he first loved us.*

2. He gives me a love for other people.
Romans 5:5 — ...*Hope does not disappoint us, because God has poured out his love into our hearts by the Holy Spirit, whom he has given us.*

3. He gives me new spiritual understanding.
I John 5:20 — *We know also that the Son of God has come and has given us understanding, so that we may know him who is true. And we are in him who is true — even in his Son Jesus Christ. He is the true God and eternal life.*

4. He gives me new power and a holy desire to do God's will.
Philippians 2:13 — ...*It is God who works in you to will and to act according to his good purpose.*

5. He gives me true peace and joy in my conscience.
Romans 5:1 — *Therefore, since we have been justified through faith, we have peace with God through our Lord Jesus Christ...*

6. He gives me a new sense of who I am.
II Corinthians 5:17 — *Therefore, if anyone is in Christ, he is a new creation; the old has gone, the new has come!*

Psalm 23:5b,6 — ...*You anoint my head with oil; my cup over-flows. Surely goodness and love will follow me all the days of my life, and I will dwell in the house of the Lord forever.*

Ephesians 2:10 — *For we are God's workmanship, created in Christ Jesus to do good works, which God prepared in advance for us to do.*

230. Who needs the new birth?

Everyone needs the new birth because all are born spiritually dead and therefore cannot enter the Kingdom of God.

John 3:6 — *"That which is born of the flesh is flesh; and that which is born of the Spirit is spirit..." (New American Standard Bible).*

231. By what means does the new birth come to a person?

The new birth comes to us by means of the Word of God and baptism.

Titus 3:4-7 — ...*When the kindness and love of God our Savior appeared, he saved us, not because of righteous things we had done, but because of his mercy. He saved us through the washing of rebirth and renewal by the Holy Spirit, whom he poured out on us generously through Jesus Christ our Savior, so that, having been justified by his grace, we might become heirs having the hope of eternal life.*

John 3:5 — *Jesus answers, "I tell you the truth, no one can enter the kingdom of God unless he is born of water and the Spirit."*

I Peter 1:23 — *For you have been born again, not of perishable seed, but of imperishable, through the living and enduring word of God.*

Romans 10:17 — *"...Faith comes from hearing the message and the message is heard through the word of Christ."*

I Peter 3:20-22 — ...*In this ark a few, that is eight persons, were saved by water. In the same way also, baptism now saves us, not by washing dirt from the body, but by guaranteeing us a good conscience before God by the resurrection of Jesus Christ, who has gone to heaven and is at the right hand of God, where angels, rulers, and powers have been put under Him (God's Word to the Nations).*

232. What is sanctification?

Sanctification is the gracious work of the Holy Spirit by which He daily renews me more and more in the image of God through the Word and Sacraments.

I Thessalonians 5:23,24 — *May God himself, the God of peace, sanctify you through and through. May your whole spirit, soul and body be kept blameless at the coming of our Lord Jesus Christ. The one who calls you is faithful and he will do it.*

Philippians 2:12,13 — *Therefore, my dear friends, as you have always obeyed — not only in my presence, but now much more in my absence — continue to work out your salvation with fear and trembling, for it is God who works in you to will and to act according to his good purpose.*

233. How does sanctification show itself in your daily life?

It is shown in a growing love for God and other people, a desire to do His will in all things, and also by self-denial in striving against the devil, the world and my own sinful human nature.

Ephesians 3:16-19 — *I pray that out of his glorious riches he may strengthen you with power through his Spirit in your inner being, so that Christ may dwell in your hearts through faith. And I pray that you, being rooted and established in love, may have power, together with all the saints, to grasp how wide and long and high and deep is the love of Christ, and to know this love that surpasses knowledge — that you may be filled to the measure of all the fullness of God.*

Colossians 2:6,7 — *So then, just as you received Christ Jesus as Lord, continue to live in him, rooted and built up in him, strengthened in the faith as you were taught, and overflowing with thankfulness.*

Matthew 16:24 — *Then Jesus said to his disciples, "If anyone would come after me, he must deny himself and take up his cross and follow me..."*

234. Do you remain saved by your own good life?

No, my Lord Jesus Christ has done everything necessary for my justification and sanctification, and I can depend completely upon Him.

I Corinthians 1:30 — "...Christ Jesus...has become for us wisdom from God —that is, our righteousness, holiness and redemption."

235. What are the fruits of a living faith?

The fruits of a living faith are good works produced by the Holy Spirit and done out of love for God, my neighbor's good, and my own true welfare.

Matthew 25:35,36 — *"For I was hungry and you gave me something to eat, I was thirsty and you gave me something to drink, I was a stranger and you invited me in, I needed clothes and you clothed me, I was sick and you looked after me, I was in prison and you came to visit me."*

I Timothy 6:18 — *Command them to do good, to be rich in good deeds, and to be generous and willing to share.*

Hebrews 10:24 — *...Let us consider how we may spur one another on toward love and good deeds.*

236. What is preservation?

Preservation is that gracious work of the Holy Spirit by which He, through the Word of God and the Lord's Supper, feeds and strengthens my spiritual life, and gives me instruction, guidance, correction and comfort, keeping me in God's grace.

Philippians 1:4,6 — *...I always pray with joy...confident of this, that he who began a good work in you will carry it on to completion until the day of Christ Jesus.*

II Timothy 3:16,17 — *All Scripture is God-breathed and is useful for teaching, rebuking, correcting and training in righteousness so that the man of God may be thoroughly equipped for every good work.*

I Peter 2:24,25 — *He himself bore our sins in his body on the tree, so that we might die to sins and live for righteousness; by his wounds you have been healed. For you were like sheep going astray, but now you have returned to the Shepherd and Overseer of your souls.*

237. What does it mean to gather the whole Christian Church?

The Holy Spirit gathers the whole Christian Church when He calls people one by one into fellowship with Christ and makes of them one family before God.

I Corinthians 12:12,13 — *The body is a unit, though it is made up of many parts; and though all its parts are many, they form one body. So it is with Christ. For we were all baptized by one Spirit into one body — whether Jews or Greeks, slave or free — and we were all given the one Spirit to drink.*

238. What is the Holy Christian Church?

The Holy Christian Church is the communion of saints, that is, all believers in Christ, since all believers, and only believers, are members of this Church.

Ephesians 2:19-22 — *Consequently, you are no longer foreigners and aliens, but fellow citizens with God's people and members of God's household, built on the foundation of the apostles and prophets, with Christ Jesus himself as the chief cornerstone. In him the whole building is joined together and rises to become a holy temple in the Lord. And in him you too are being built together to become a dwelling in which God lives by his Spirit.*

Romans 12:4,5 — *Just as each of us has one body with many members, and these members do not all have the same function, so in Christ we who are many form one body, and each member belongs to all the others.*

Romans 8:9b — *If anyone does not have the Spirit of Christ, he does not belong to Christ.*

239. What does the Bible teach about the way the Church began?

The Bible teaches that the Church began when the Holy Spirit was given to all believers on the Day of Pentecost, ten days after Christ's ascension to heaven.

Acts 2:41,42 — *Those who accepted his message were baptized, and about three thousand were added to their number that day. They devoted themselves to the apostles' teaching and to the fellowship, to the breaking of bread and to prayer.*

240. Why do you say "I believe in the Holy Christian Church"?

I say *"I believe* in the Holy Christian Church," because I know from God's Word that this church exists, even though I cannot determine with certainty who its members are; and because I know that His church will always continue.

Matthew 16:18-19 — *"...On this rock I will build my church, and the gates of Hades will not overcome it. I will give you the keys of the kingdom of heaven; whatever you bind on earth will be bound in heaven, and whatever you loose on earth will be loosed in heaven."*

241. Why do you say, "The Holy Christian Church"?

I say, *"The* Holy Christian Church" because the true Church is one spiritual body, of which Christ is the head.
II Timothy 2:19a — *Nevertheless, God's solid foundation stands firm, sealed with this inscription: "The Lord knows those who are his,..."*
Luke 17:20-21 — *Once, having been asked by the Pharisees when the kingdom of God would come, Jesus replied, "The kingdom of God does not come with your careful observation, nor will people say, 'Here it is', or 'There it is', because the kingdom of God is within you."*

242. Why do you say, "Holy Christian Church"?

I say, *"Holy* Christian Church" because the Holy Spirit lives and works in this communion of believers and because it is made up of those who have responded to God's call and seek to live their lives according to God's will as found in the Scriptures.
Titus 2:13b,14 — *...Jesus Christ...gave himself for us to redeem us from all wickedness and to purify for himself a people that are his very own, eager to do what is good.*
John 16:7 — *"...I tell you the truth: It is for your good that I am going away. Unless I go away, the Counselor will not come to you, but if I go, I will send him to you..."*

243. Why do you say, "Christian Church"?

I say, *"Christian* Church" because the Church belongs to Christ and is built upon Him as its only foundation.

244. Why is the Church called catholic in some of the Christian creeds?

The Church is called *catholic,* or *universal,* because God invited all people to enter it, and because it is to be found in all parts of the world where the Gospel is preached.

245. How is this Church visible in the world?

The Church is visible in this world when Christians unite around the Word and Sacraments and form congregations. These congregations may be organized into synods, denominations, or associations.

Acts 2:47b — *And the Lord added to their number daily those who were being saved.*

246. Why do Christians unite in this way?

Christians unite in this way in order that the Gospel might be preached in purity and the sacraments administered according to the Gospel.

Hebrews 10:25 — *Let us not give up meeting together, as some are in the habit of doing, but let us encourage one another — and all the more as you see the Day approaching.*

Ephesians 4:11-13 — *It was he [Christ] who gave some to be apostles, some to be prophets, some to be evangelists, and some to be pastors and teachers, to prepare God's people for works of service, so that the body of Christ may be built up until we all reach unity in the faith and in the knowledge of the Son of God and become mature, attaining to the whole measure of the fullness of Christ.*

Colossians 3:16 — *Let the word of Christ dwell in you richly as you teach and admonish one another with all wisdom, and as you sing psalms, hymns and spiritual songs with gratitude in your hearts to God.*

247. Why is it important for you to be a member of a congregation?

It is important for me to be a member of a congregation because:

1. It means that I publicly declare that I am a Christian and therefore part of Christ's body, the Church.

2. It means that as part of the body of Christ I support it with my loyalty, offerings, and spiritual gifts.

3. It means that I have submitted to the Lordship of Christ, as exercised by the shepherding of the pastor and elders of the

congregation and am willing to submit to the congregation's teaching and spiritual guidance.

248. Who may be a member of a congregation of Christian people?

Anyone who has been baptized, who confesses faith in Christ as Savior, and who follows the procedures for membership in a particular congregation may be a member.

249. How should church members behave in their daily lives?

Church members should live in such a way that they honor God by a holy life, show love to others, as Jesus taught, and tell the good news of salvation to the world.

I Peter 2:11,12 — *Dear friends, I urge you, as aliens and strangers in the world, to abstain from sinful desires which war against your soul. Live such good lives among the pagans that, though they accuse you of doing wrong, they may see your good deeds and glorify God on the day he visits us.*

I John 3:10,11 — *This is how we know who the children of God are and who the children of the devil are: Anyone who does not do what is right is not a child of God; nor is anyone who does not love his brother. This is the message you heard from the beginning. We should love one another.*

Romans 13:14 — *...Clothe yourselves with the Lord Jesus Christ, and do not think about how to gratify the desires of the sinful nature.*

Galatians 5:16 — *So I say, live by the Spirit, and you will not gratify the desires of the sinful nature.*

John 13:34,35 — *"A new command I give you: Love one another. As I have loved you, so you must love one another. By this all men will know that you are my disciples, if you love one another."*

Acts 1:8 — *"...But you will receive power when the Holy Spirit comes on you; and you will be my witnesses in Jerusalem, and in all Judea and Samaria, and to the ends of the earth."*

250. Do congregations always consist only of those who have a living faith in Jesus Christ?

No, there may be those who confess faith in Christ as Savior but who do not truly believe in Him. The Bible calls such people hypocrites.

Titus 1:16 — *They claim to know God, but by their actions they deny him. They are detestable, disobedient and unfit for doing anything good.*

Luke 6:46 — *"Why do you call me, Lord, Lord, and do not do what I say?..."*

Isaiah 29:13 — *The Lord says: "These people come near to me with their mouth and honor me with their lips, but their hearts are far from me. Their worship of me is made up only of rules taught by men..."*

251. What does the Bible say about how the church should deal with members who will not turn away from their sin?

The Bible says, "I have written you in my letter not to associate with sexually immoral people — not at all meaning the people of this world who are immoral, or the greedy and swindlers, or idolaters. In that case you would have to leave this world. But now I am writing you that you must not associate with anyone who calls himself a brother but is sexually immoral or greedy, an idolater or a slanderer, a drunkard or a swindler. With such a man do not even eat.

"What business is it of mine to judge those outside the church? Are you not to judge those inside? God will judge those outside. 'Expel the wicked man from among you'" (I Corinthians 5:9-13).

252. Where does the church get its authority to do this?

The church gets its authority to do this from the words of Jesus. Matthew 18:18 — *"I tell you the truth, whatever you bind on earth will be bound in heaven, and whatever you loose on earth will be loosed in heaven."*

253. What does the Bible say about what your attitude should be toward those who are caught in acts of sin?

The Bible says, "Brothers, if someone is caught in a sin, you who are spiritual should restore him gently. But watch yourself, or you also may be tempted. Carry each other's burdens, and in this way you will fulfill the law of Christ" (Galatians 6:1,2).

254. What shall the congregation do when the expelled person repents of sin?

The congregation shall forgive the person who repents and restore that person to membership in the church.

II Corinthians 2:7b,8 — *You ought to forgive and comfort him so that he will not be overwhelmed by excessive sorrow. I urge you, therefore, to reaffirm your love for him.*

255. What does Jesus say about how you should deal with other Christians who do wrong things to you?

Jesus says, "If your brother sins against you, go and show him his fault, just between the two of you. If he listens to you, you have won your brother over. But if he will not listen, take one or two others along, so that every matter may be established by the testimony of two or three witnesses. If he refuses to listen to them, tell it to the church; and if he refuses to listen even to the church, treat him as you would a pagan or a tax collector" (Matthew 18:15-17).

256. What mission has Christ given His Church to do?

Christ has commanded His Church to "...Go and make disciples of all nations, baptizing them in the name of the Father and of the Son and of the Holy Spirit, and teaching them to obey everything I have commanded you" (Matthew 28:19,20a).

Acts 1:8 — *"...You will receive power when the Holy Spirit comes on you; and you will be my witnesses in Jerusalem, and in all Judea and Samaria, and to the ends of the earth."*

257. How is this mission to be carried out?

Christ's mission is to be carried out by Christians who use the gifts which the Holy Spirit has given to members of the body of Christ.

I Peter 4:10,11 — *Each one should use whatever gift he has received to serve others, faithfully administering God's grace in its various forms. If anyone speaks, he should do it as one speaking the very words of God. If anyone serves, he should do it with the strength God provides, so that in all things God may be praised through Jesus Christ. To him be the glory and the power for ever and ever. Amen.*

258. What gifts has the Holy Spirit given to believers in His Church?

The Holy Spirit has given many different gifts to His Church in order that the members of the church, like the parts of a body, may work together for the good of the whole church.

I Corinthians 12:4-6 — *There are different kinds of gifts, but the same Spirit. There are different kinds of service, but the same Lord. There are different kinds of working, but the same God works all of them in all men.*

Romans 12:5-8 — *...In Christ we who are many form one body, and each member belongs to all the others. We have different gifts, according to the grace given us. If a man's gift is prophesying, let him use it in proportion to his faith. If it is serving, let him serve; if it is teaching, let him teach; if it is encouraging, let him encourage; if it is contributing to the needs of others, let him give generously; if it is leadership, let him govern diligently; if it is showing mercy, let him do it cheerfully.*

Ephesians 4:11-13 — *It was he who gave some to be apostles, some to be prophets, some to be evangelists, and some to be pastors and teachers, to prepare God's people for works of service, so that the body of Christ may be built up until we all reach unity in the faith and in the knowledge of the Son of God and become mature, attaining to the whole measure of the fullness of Christ.*

259. How can you have a part in this mission?

I can willingly offer myself to be used by God in whatever way He wants.

Romans 12:1,2 — *Therefore, I urge you, brothers, in view of God's mercy, to offer your bodies as living sacrifices, holy and pleasing to God — this is your spiritual act of worship. Do not conform any longer to the pattern of this world, but be transformed by the renewing of your mind. Then you will be able to test and approve what God's will is — his good, pleasing and perfect will.*

260. What does the Holy Spirit give to you in the Christian Church?

In the Christian Church He daily forgives all my sins, and the sins of all other believers.

John 20:21b-23 — *"As the Father has sent me, I am sending you." And with that he breathed on them and said, "Receive the Holy Spirit. If you forgive anyone his sins, they are forgiven; if you do not forgive them, they are not forgiven."*

Acts 13:38 — *"Therefore, my brothers, I want you to know that through Jesus the forgiveness of sins is proclaimed to you."*

I John 1:9 — *If we confess our sins, he is faithful and just and will forgive us our sins and purify us from all unrighteousness.*

261. Why does a believer need the daily forgiveness of sins?

Daily forgiveness is needed because a believer has a sinful nature and sins every day.

I John 1:8 — *If we claim to be without sin, we deceive ourselves and the truth is not in us.*

262. How may a believer live in the daily forgiveness of sins?

A believer may live in daily forgiveness of sins by admitting them, confessing them honestly to God, and willingly forsaking them.

Proverbs 28:13 — *He who conceals his sins does not prosper, but whoever confesses and renounces them finds mercy.*

263. What are the results of the daily forgiveness of sins?

The daily forgiveness of sins brings peace and confidence to the believer.

Matthew 11:28,29 — *"Come to me, all you who are weary and burdened, and I will give you rest. Take my yoke upon you and learn from me, for I am gentle and humble in heart, and you will find rest for your souls."*

264. When will a believer be entirely free from sin?

A believer will be entirely free from sin only after leaving this life and entering the presence of God.

I John 3:2 — *Dear friends, now we are children of God, and what we will be has not yet been made known. But we know that when he appears, we shall be like him, for we shall see him as he is.*

265. What becomes of a believer after death?

The believer goes home to God, where there is rest from all trouble and sorrow in happy fellowship with God until the resurrection of the body.

Luke 23:43 — *Jesus answered him, "I tell you the truth, today you will be with me in paradise."*

Revelation 14:13 — *"Blessed are the dead who die in the Lord...they will rest from their labor..."*

266. What do you mean by the resurrection of the body?

By the resurrection of the body I mean that my dead body will one day be made alive and will be with Christ where He is forever.

John 5:28,29 — *"Do not be amazed at this, for a time is coming when all who are in their graves will hear his voice and come out — those who have done good will rise to live, and those who have done evil will rise to be condemned."*

Romans 8:11 — *And if the Spirit of him who raised Jesus from the dead is living in you, he who raised Christ from the dead will also give life to your mortal bodies through his Spirit, who lives in you.*

John 11:25 — *Jesus said to her, "I am the resurrection and the life. He who believes in me will live, even though he dies; and whoever lives and believes in me will never die..."*

I Corinthians 15:51,52 — *Listen, I tell you a mystery: We will not all sleep, but we will all be changed — in a flash, in the twinkling of an eye, at the last trumpet. For the trumpet will sound, the dead will be raised imperishable, and we will be changed.*

267. What change will then take place in your body and the bodies of all other believers?

My body and the bodies of all other believers will become like the body of the risen Christ which will never die again.

Philippians 3:20,21 — *Our citizenship is in heaven. And we eagerly await a Savior from there, the Lord Jesus Christ, who, by the power that enables him to bring everything under his control, will transform our lowly bodies so that they will be like his glorious body.*

I Corinthians 15:42-44a — *So will it be with the resurrection of the dead. The body that is sown is perishable, it is raised imperishable; it is sown in dishonor, it is raised in glory; it is sown in weakness, it is raised in power; it is sown a natural body, it is raised a spiritual body.*

268. What will happen to those who reject Jesus as Savior?

Those who reject Jesus as Savior will be condemned to eternal death.

Matthew 25:41,46 — *"Then he will say to those on his left, Depart from me, you who are cursed, into the eternal fire prepared for the devil and his angels...Then they will go away to eternal punishment, but the righteous to eternal life."*

269. What is eternal death?

Eternal death is a dreadful separation from God which will last forever.

Matthew 13:40-42 — *"As the weeds are pulled up and burned in the fire, so it will be at the end of the age. The Son of Man will send out his angels, and they will weed out of his kingdom everything that causes sin and all who do evil. They will throw them into the fiery furnace, where there will be weeping and gnashing of teeth. Then the righteous will shine like the sun in the kingdom of their Father. He who has ears, let him hear."*

Daniel 12:2 — *Multitudes who sleep in the dust of the earth will awake: some to everlasting life, others to shame and everlasting contempt.*

270. Who will be condemned in this way?

All who do not repent of sin and trust in Jesus as Savior will be condemned.

Acts 4:12 — *Salvation is found in no one else, for there is no other name under heaven given to men by which we must be saved.*

John 3:36 — *"Whoever believes in the Son has eternal life, but whoever rejects the Son will not see life, for God's wrath remains on him."*

271. How can you have eternal life?

I can have eternal life by continually receiving the grace that God offers me in the Gospel.

John 17:3 — *"Now this is eternal life: that they may know you, the only true God, and Jesus Christ, whom you have sent."*

Philippians 3:8,9 — *...I consider everything a loss compared to the surpassing greatness of knowing Christ Jesus my Lord, for whose sake I have lost all things. I consider them rubbish, that I may gain Christ and be found in him, not having a righteousness of my own that comes from the law, but that which is through faith in Christ — the righteousness that comes from God and is by faith.*

272. What does the word *Amen* mean at the end of the Apostles' Creed?

The word *Amen* means *so be it* and is used to emphasize the truth of the creed that I confess.

The Lord's Prayer

Our Father, who art in heaven, Hallowed be thy name; Thy kingdom come. Thy will be done in earth as it is in heaven. Give us this day our daily bread. And forgive us our trespasses, as we forgive those who trespass against us. And lead us not into temptation, but deliver us from evil. For thine is the kingdom, and the power, and the glory, forever. Amen.

Our Father in heaven, hallowed be your name, your kingdom come, your will be done on earth as it is in heaven. Give us today our daily bread. Forgive us our debts, as we also have forgiven our debtors. And lead us not into temptation, but deliver us from the evil one, for yours is the kingdom and the power and the glory forever. Amen (Matthew 6:9-13, *New International Version.*)

273. Why has Jesus given you this prayer?

Jesus has given me this prayer to show me what true prayer is, and to teach me as God's child how to speak to my heavenly Father.

274. What other divine person helps you to pray?

The Holy Spirit helps me to pray, and He prays for me.
Romans 8:26,27 — *...The Spirit helps us in our weakness. We do not know what we ought to pray for, but the Spirit himself intercedes for us with groans that words cannot express. And he who searches our hearts knows the mind of the Spirit, because the Spirit intercedes for the saints in accordance with God's will.*

275. What is prayer?

Prayer is talking to God silently or aloud from my heart.

276. In whose name should you pray?

I should pray in the name of Jesus.
John 16:24 — *"Until now you have not asked for anything in my name. Ask and you will receive, and your joy will be complete."*

277. What does it mean to pray in the name of Jesus?

To pray in the name of Jesus means:
1. That I base my prayer on what Jesus did when He, through His death, opened up the way to God.

2. That I am praying according to what Jesus wants for me and the whole world.

278. When should you pray?

Since God is always ready to hear me when I pray, I should have regular times of prayer alone and with other Christians, and always have an attitude of prayer as I think about my Father who is in heaven.
I Thessalonians 5:17 — *Pray continually.*
Ephesians 6:18 — *Pray in the Spirit on all occasions with all kinds of prayers and requests.*
Matthew 6:6a — *"...When you pray, go into your room, close the door and pray to your Father, who is unseen."*

279. For whom should you pray?

I should pray for myself and the whole world, even my enemies.
I Timothy 2:1,2 — *I urge, then, first of all, that requests, prayers, intercession and thanksgiving be made for everyone — for kings and all those in authority, that we may live peaceful lives in all godliness and holiness.*
Matthew 5:44,45a — *"...I tell you: Love your enemies and pray for those who persecute you, that you may be sons of your Father in heaven."*

280. For what should I pray?

I should pray for the will of God to be done.

281. Does God always answer your prayers?

Yes, He always does when I pray according to His will.
Ephesians 3:20,21— *Now to him who is able to do immeasurably more than all we ask or imagine, according to his power that is at work within us, to him be glory in the church and in Christ Jesus throughout all generations, for ever and ever! Amen.*
John 15:7 —*"If you remain in me and my words remain in you, ask whatever you wish, and it will be given you."*

282. Is God's answer sometimes "no"?

Yes, God sometimes withholds what I ask for because I may ask with wrong motives and because He knows what is best for me.
James 4:3 — *When you ask, you do not receive, because you ask with wrong motives, that you may spend what you get on your pleasures.*
II Corinthians 12:8,9— *Three times I pleaded with the Lord to take it away from me. But he said to me, "My grace is sufficient for you, for my power is made perfect in weakness." Therefore I will boast all the more gladly about my weaknesses, so that Christ's power may rest on me.*

283. Are all your prayers answered right away?

No, some prayers are answered right away, but at other times God, in His wisdom, delays the answer.
Psalm 40:1 —*I waited patiently for the Lord; he turned to me and heard my cry.*
Jeremiah 33:3— *"Call to me and I will answer you and tell you great and unsearchable things you do not know."*
James 5:16b—*The prayer of a righteous man is powerful and effective.*

Our Father in heaven.

What does this mean?

With these words God tenderly invites us to believe that He is our true Father and that we are His true children, so that we may pray to Him as boldly and confidently as dear children ask their dear father.

284. How does Jesus teach you to address God in the Lord's Prayer?

He teaches me to speak to God as my heavenly Father.

285. What does this mean to you?

To have God as my heavenly Father means that I am His child and therefore can confidently come to Him in prayer.
Psalm 68:5,6a — *A father to the fatherless, a defender of widows, is God in his holy dwelling. God sets the lonely in families...*

286. Who can call God their Father?

Those who believe in Jesus as Savior can call God their Father.
Galatians 4:6 — *Because you are sons, God sent the Spirit of his Son into our hearts, the Spirit who calls out, "Abba Father."*

287. Why does Jesus teach you to pray, *Our* Father?

I am to pray *Our* Father, because I am to pray with and for others and because it reminds me that I belong to a family of believers who together confess God as Father.
Ephesians 6:18 — *Pray in the Spirit on all occasions with all kinds of prayers and requests. With this in mind, be alert and always keep on praying for all the saints.*

288. Why does Jesus teach you to pray "Our Father in heaven"?

These words are to remind me that my heavenly Father is exalted in love and power above all earthly fathers.
Matthew 7:11 — *"If you, then, though you are evil, know how to give good gifts to your children, how much more will your Father in heaven give good gifts to those who ask him!"*
Ephesians 3:14,15 — *For this reason I kneel before the Father, from whom his whole family in heaven and earth derives its name.*

The First Petition

Hallowed be your name.

What does this mean?

God's name is holy in itself, but we pray that it may be holy also among us.

How is this done?

It is made holy when the Word of God is taught in its truth and purity, and when we, as God's children, live holy lives in accordance with it. This grant us, dear Father in heaven! But whoever teaches and lives in a way other than what the Word of God teaches, profanes the name of God among us. From this preserve us, heavenly Father.

289. What do you pray for in the first petition?

I pray in this petition that the name of God may be considered holy and be honored by all people.
Psalm 72:19 — *Praise be to his glorious name forever; may the whole earth be filled with his glory.*

290. When is the name of God hallowed or honored?

God's name is honored when the Word of God is taught truthfully and purely and when we gladly hear and obey it.
Acts 17:11 — *Now the Bereans were of more noble character than the Thessalonians, for they received the message with great eagerness and examined the Scriptures every day to see if what Paul said was true.*

I Peter 4:11a — *If anyone speaks, he should do it as one speaking the very words of God.*

James 2:22 — *You see that his [Abraham's] faith and his actions were working together, and his faith was made complete by what he did.*

291. When do you profane the name of God?

I profane the name of God if I teach and live in a manner contrary to the Word of God.

I John 1:6 — *If we claim to have fellowship with him yet walk in the darkness, we lie and do not live by the truth.*

292. How can you honor God's name in the meetings of the church?

I can honor God's name by preparing my own heart before the meeting, and by quietly and reverently waiting for God to speak to me as I gladly hear His Word and sing His praises.

Psalm 46:10a — *Be still, and know that I am God...*

Psalm 122:1 — *I was glad when they said to me, "Let us go to the house of the Lord!" (Revised Standard Version)*

The Second Petition

Your kingdom come.

What does this mean?

The kingdom of God truly does come of itself, without our prayer, but we pray in this petition that it may also come to us.

How is this done?

The kingdom of God comes to us when our heavenly Father gives us His Holy Spirit, so that by His grace we believe His Holy Word, and live a godly life here on earth and in heaven forever.

293. What is meant in this petition by the kingdom of God?

The kingdom of God is the kingdom of grace in which God rules in the hearts and lives of believers and which one day will become the kingdom of glory in heaven where those who are saved are with Christ in perfect happiness forever.

Romans 14:17 — *For the kingdom of God is not a matter of eating and drinking, but of righteousness, peace and joy in the Holy Spirit.*

Luke 17:20b,21 — *"The kingdom of God does not come with your careful observation, nor will people say, Here it is, or There it is, because the kingdom of God is within you."*

Colossians 1:13,14 — *For he [God] has rescued us from the dominion of darkness and brought us into the kingdom of the Son he loves, in whom we have redemption, the forgiveness of sins.*

294. Why do we pray, "Your kingdom come"?

1. We pray this because we cannot enter God's kingdom of grace by our own power, but it must come to us.
John 6:44 — *"No one can come to me unless the Father who sent me draws him..."*

2. We pray this because we want God's kingdom of grace to come to all people everywhere.
I Timothy 2:3-6a — *This is good, and pleases God our Savior, who wants all men to be saved and to come to a knowledge of the truth. For there is one God and one mediator between God and men, the man Christ Jesus, who gave himself as a ransom for all men...*
Matthew 9:38 — *"...Ask the Lord of the harvest, therefore, to send out workers into his harvest field."*

3. We pray this because we want Jesus to return to begin His kingdom of glory.
Revelation 22:20 — *He who testifies to these things says, "Yes, I am coming soon."*

295. When does the kingdom of God come to a person?

The kingdom of God comes when our heavenly Father gives the Holy Spirit and a person is given the power to believe in Jesus.
John 3:5-6 — *Jesus answered, "I tell you the truth, no one can enter the kingdom of God unless he is born of water and the Spirit. Flesh gives birth to flesh, but the Spirit gives birth to spirit..."*
Ephesians 2:8-10 — *For it is by grace you have been saved, through faith — and this not from yourselves, it is the gift of God — not by works, so that no one can boast.*

296. Can the kingdom of God come even to a little child?

Certainly! Jesus said that adults must become like little children to enter the kingdom of God.
Luke 18:16,17 — *...Jesus called the children to him and said, "Let the little children come to me, and do not hinder them, for the kingdom of God belongs to such as these. I tell you the truth, anyone who will not receive the kingdom of God like a little child will never enter it.*

297. When will this petition be completely answered?

This petition will be completely answered when believers are in heaven with Jesus forever in perfect happiness.

II Peter 3:13,14 — *...In keeping with his promise we are looking forward to a new heaven and a new earth, the home of righteousness. So then, dear friends, since you are looking forward to this, make every effort to be found spotless, blameless and at peace with him.*

Revelation 11:15 — *"The kingdom of the world has become the kingdom of our Lord and of his Christ, and he will reign for ever and ever."*

298. To what kingdom do those belong who love and serve sin?

They belong to the kingdom of Satan.

I John 3:8 — *...The one who practices sin is of the devil; for the devil has sinned from the beginning. The Son of God appeared for this purpose, that He might destroy the works of the devil (New American Standard Bible).*

John 8:44 — *"You belong to your father, the devil, and you want to carry out your father's desire. He was a murderer from the beginning, not holding to the truth, for there is no truth in him. When he lies, he speaks his native language, for he is a liar and the father of lies."*

The Third Petition

Your will be done on earth as it is in heaven.

What does this mean?

The good and gracious will of God is done without our prayer; but we pray in this petition that it may also be done among us.

How is this done?

The good and gracious will of God is done when God destroys and brings to nothing every evil counsel and purpose of Satan, the world, and our own human nature, which would hinder us from hallowing His name and prevent the coming of His Kingdom, and when He strengthens us and keeps us steadfast in His Word and in faith, even to the end.

299. **What do we pray for in the third petition?**

We pray that we and all people on earth may do God's will.

300. **What is the will of God?**

The will of God is that His name shall be hallowed and that His kingdom come to us.
John 6:40 — *"For my Father's will is that everyone who looks to the Son and believes in him shall have eternal life..."*
I Thessalonians 4:3-8 — *For this is the will of God, your sanctification: that you abstain from fornication; that each one of you know how to control your own body in holiness and honor, not with lustful passion, like the Gentiles who do not know God; that*

no one wrong or exploit a brother or sister in this matter, because the Lord is an avenger in all these things, just as we have already told you before-hand and solemnly warned you. For God did not call us to impurity but in holiness. Therefore whoever rejects this rejects not human authority but God, who also gives his Holy Spirit to you (New Revised Standard Version Bible).

301. Where is the will of God done perfectly?

The will of God is done perfectly in heaven, where there is no hatred, sorrow, pain, injustice, hunger, war or persecution, and where everyone loves God and does His will.

302. When is the will of God done among us?

God's will is done among us, His church, when we love God and love others, as He loves us.
John 13:34,35 — *"A new command I give you: Love one another. As I have loved you, so you must love one another. By this all men will know that you are my disciples, if you love one another."*

303. What enemies seek to prevent the will of God from being done?

Satan, the world, and our own human nature seek to prevent God's will from being done.
Ephesians 6:12 — *For our struggle is not against flesh and blood, but against the rulers, against the authorities, against the powers of this dark world and against the spiritual forces of evil in the heavenly realms.*
Titus 2:11-14 — *For the grace of God that brings salvation has appeared to all men. It teaches us to say "No" to ungodliness and worldly passions, and to live self-controlled, upright and godly lives in this present age, while we wait for the blessed hope — the glorious appearing of our great God and Savior, Jesus Christ, who gave himself for us to redeem us from all wickedness and to purify for himself a people that are his very own, eager to do what is good.*

The Fourth Petition

Give us today our daily bread.

What is meant by this?

God truly does give daily bread to all, even to the wicked, without our prayer; but we pray in this petition that He would make us aware that these gifts come from Him as a gift and enable us to receive these gifts with thanksgiving.

What is meant by daily bread?

By daily bread we mean everything that is required to satisfy our bodily needs, such as food and clothing, house and home, fields and flocks, money and property, pious parents and children, trustworthy servants, godly and faithful rulers, good government, seasonable weather, peace and health, order and honor, true friends, good neighbors, and the like.

304. Does God give you daily bread only when you ask for it?

No, he gives me daily bread even when I do not ask Him for it and when I do not receive it with thanksgiving.
Matthew 5:45b — *"He causes his sun to rise on the evil and the good, and send rain on the righteous and the unrighteous."*
Psalm 145:15,16 — *The eyes of all look to you, and you give them their food at the proper time. You open your hand and satisfy the desires of every living thing.*

305. How should you receive your daily bread?

I should receive it as a gift from God, with prayer for His blessing, and thanksgiving for His goodness.

James 1:17a — *Every good and perfect gift is from above...*

I Corinthians 10:31 — *So whether you eat or drink or whatever you do, do it all for the glory of God.*

Ephesians 5:19b,20 — *Sing and make music in your heart to the Lord, always giving thanks to God the Father for everything, in the name of our Lord Jesus Christ.*

306. Why do you pray for daily bread?

Jesus teaches me to pray for daily bread because He wants me to learn to be content with what He gives me each day and not to worry about the future.

Proverbs 30:8b — *...Give me neither poverty nor riches, but give me only my daily bread.*

I Timothy 6:6 — *...Godliness with contentment is great gain.*

Matthew 6:34 — *"...Do not worry about tomorrow, for tomorrow will worry about itself. Each day has enough trouble of its own."*

307. Must you work for your daily bread when you pray for it every day?

Yes, God wants me to be hardworking, so that I do not take advantage of other people's generosity, but seek to earn a living through willing and honest work.

Genesis 3:19 — *"...By the sweat of your brow you will eat your food until you return to the ground, since from it you were taken; for dust you are and to dust you will return."*

II Thessalonians 3:10b — *We gave you this rule: "If a man will not work, he shall not eat."*

308. What is your duty to those who have no daily bread?

My duty to those who have no daily bread is to feed them.

James 2:15-17 — *Suppose a brother or sister is without clothes and daily food. If one of you says to him, "Go, I wish you well; keep warm and well fed," but does nothing about his physical needs, what good is it?*

Isaiah 58:10 — *If you spend yourselves in behalf of the hungry and satisfy the needs of the oppressed, then your light will rise in the darkness, and your night will become like the noonday.*
Ezekiel 18:5,7b — *"Suppose there is a righteous man who does what is just and right...He...gives his food to the hungry and provides clothing for the naked..."*
Ephesians 4:28 — *He who has been stealing must steal no longer, but must work, doing something useful with his own hands, that he may have something to share with those in need.*

The Fifth Petition

Forgive us our debts, as we also have forgiven our debtors.

What does this mean?
We pray in this petition that our heavenly Father would not look upon our sins nor deny our prayers because of them, for we neither merit nor are worthy of those things for which we pray. However, we pray that He would grant us all things through His grace, even though we daily sin and deserve nothing but punishment. And certainly, on our part, we will gladly forgive and cheerfully do good to those who may sin against us.

309. What do you pray for in the fifth petition?

I pray that God will forgive my sins.

310. What is meant by the word debts or the word trespasses?

These words mean *all my daily sin and imperfection.*
James 3:2a — *We all stumble in many ways.*

311. How can you be certain of God's forgiveness?

I can be certain of God's forgiveness because He has said in the
Bible that He will forgive my sins.
I John 2:1 — *My dear children, I write this to you so that you will
not sin. But if anybody does sin, we have one who speaks to the
Father in our defense — Jesus Christ, the Righteous One.*
I John 5:14,15 — *This is the confidence we have in approaching
God; that if we ask anything according to his will, he hears us.
And if we know that he hears us — whatever we ask — we know
that we have what we asked of him.*

312. For whose sake does God forgive your sin?

God forgives me, not for my sake because I ask in the right way,
but for Jesus' sake, who died for me and rose again and who is
now in the presence of the Father praying for me.
Ephesians 1:7 — *"In him [Jesus] we have redemption through
his blood, the forgiveness of sins, in accordance with the riches
of God's grace...*
Hebrews 7:25 — *Therefore he [Jesus] is able to save completely
those who come to God through him, because he always lives to
intercede for them.*

**313. What does Jesus say is necessary in order for you to be
forgiven?**

Jesus says that in order for me to be forgiven, it is necessary for
me to forgive anyone who sins against me.
Luke 6:37c — *"Forgive, and you will be forgiven."*
Matthew 6:15 — *"...If you do not forgive men their sins, your
Father will not forgive your sins."*

314. How many times should you forgive someone?

I should remember that Jesus said there is no limit to the number
of times I forgive others.

Matthew 18:21-22 — *Then Peter came to Jesus and asked, "Lord, how many times shall I forgive my brother when he sins against me? Up to seven times?" Jesus answered, "I tell you, not seven times, but seventy-seven times."*

315. Once you have received God's grace, must you continue to ask God for forgiveness?

Yes, since I sin daily because of my human weakness, I need to be forgiven daily.

I John 1:7-9 — *If we walk in the light, as he is in the light, we have fellowship with one another, and the blood of Jesus, his Son purifies us from all sin. If we claim to be without sin, we deceive ourselves and the truth is not in us. If we confess our sins, he is faithful and just and will forgive us our sins and purify us from all unrighteousness.*

The Sixth Petition

And lead us not into temptation.

What does this mean?

God tempts no one to sin, but we pray in this petition that He would so guard and preserve us, that the devil, the world, and our own human nature may not deceive us nor lead us into error and unbelief, despair and other great and shameful sins; but when tempted, we may finally prevail and gain the victory.

316. What kinds of temptation does the Bible speak about?

The Bible speaks of two kinds. There are the trials or tests from God which He allows to come to me to strengthen my faith; and there are the enticements to do evil which come to me from Satan, the world, and my own human nature.

317. In what way is the word *temptation* used in the Sixth Petition?

In this petition the word *temptation* means *enticements to do evil.*

318. How does Satan tempt you?

Satan tempts me by trying to deceive me into distrusting God.

319. How does the world tempt you?

The world tempts me by pressures, intimidation, enticements, and bad examples to live for myself without considering God or His Word.

Proverbs 1:10 — *My son, if sinners entice you, do not give in to them.*

James 4:4b — *Anyone who chooses to be a friend of the world becomes an enemy of God.*

I John 2:15,16 — *Do not love the world or anything in the world. If anyone loves the world, the love of the Father is not in him. For everything in the world — the cravings of sinful man, the lust of his eyes and the boasting of what he has and does — comes not from the Father but from the world.*

320. What do you mean by the world?

The world is not the physical world in which I live but the satanic kingdom made up of all who oppose God and which is ruled by Satan.

Ephesians 6:12 — *For our struggle is not against flesh and blood, but against the rulers, against the authorities, against the powers of this dark world and against the spiritual forces of evil in the heavenly realms.*

321. How does your human nature tempt you?

My own human nature tempts me by evil desires of all kinds.

James 1:14 — ...*Each one is tempted when, by his own evil desire, he is dragged away and enticed.*

322. What do you mean by your human nature?

By human nature I do not mean my physical body, which is created by God, but my inner self, which is fallen and naturally wants to sin.

Romans 8:5 — *Those who live according to the sinful nature have their minds set on what that nature desires; but those who live in accordance with the Spirit have their minds set on what the Spirit desires.*

323. Can you ever be free from temptation in this world?

No, not as long as Satan, the world, and my own human nature tempt me to sin.

324. How can you prepare yourself to face temptation?

I can prepare myself to face temptation by hiding God's Word in my heart, by praying, by occupying myself with worthwhile activities, by feeding my mind with good and creative ideas, and by choosing friends who are good examples.

Philippians 4:8,9 — *...Whatever is true, whatever is noble, whatever is right, whatever is pure, whatever is lovely, whatever is admirable — if anything is excellent or praiseworthy — think about such things. Whatever you have learned or received or heard from me, or seen in me — put it into practice. And the God of peace will be with you.*

Psalm 119:9,11 — *How can a young man keep his way pure? By living according to your word...I have hidden your word in my heart that I might not sin against you.*

325. When will you be free from temptation?

I will be free from temptation when I die and am at home in heaven with God.

Revelation 21:4 — *"...He will wipe every tear from their eyes. There will be no more death or mourning or crying or pain, for the old order of things has passed away."*

Philippians 3:20,21 — *...Our citizenship is in heaven. And we eagerly await a Savior from there, the Lord Jesus Christ, who by the power that enables him to bring everything under his control, will transform our lowly bodies so that they will be like his glorious body.*

326. What can you do when you are tempted?

1. I can remember that God is all-powerful and that He loves me and has promised never to leave me.
I Corinthians 10:13 — *No temptation has seized you except what is common to man. And God is faithful; he will not let you be tempted beyond what you can bear. But when you are tempted, he will also provide a way out so that you can stand up under it.*

2. I can be on my guard and pray.
Matthew 26:41 — *"Watch and pray so that you will not fall into temptation. The spirit is willing, but the body is weak."*

3. I can walk daily in the light of God's Word and defend myself with it.
Psalm 119:9,11 — *How can a young man keep his way pure? By living according to your word...I have hidden your word in my heart that I might not sin against you.*
Ephesians 6:13 — *Therefore put on the full armor of God, so that when the day of evil comes, you may be able to stand your ground, and after you have done everything, to stand.*

The Seventh Petition

Deliver us from the evil one.

What does this mean?

We pray in this petition, as in a summary, that our heavenly Father would deliver us from the evil one, whether he affects body or soul, property or reputation, and that at last when the hour of death shall come, God may grant us a blessed end and graciously take us from this world of sorrow to Himself in heaven.

Conclusion of the Lord's Prayer

For yours is the kingdom and the power, and the glory, forever. Amen.

327. What do you learn from the doxology at the end of the Lord's Prayer?

I learn that all glory belongs to God alone and that He is able to answer my prayer.

328. What does the word *Amen* mean?

The word *Amen* is an expression of certainty, meaning *so be it,* and when used at the end of this prayer, shows that these petitions are acceptable to my Father in heaven and are heard by Him.

329. Does God hear only this prayer?

No, God hears every prayer offered according to His will.
Matthew 7:7 — *Ask and it will be given to you; seek and you will find; knock and the door will be opened to you.*
I John 5:14 — *This is the confidence we have in approaching God: that if we ask anything according to his will, he hears us.*

The Sacraments

330. How does God give His grace to you?

God has three means (or ways) of giving His grace to me: The Word of God and the two sacraments. These are the three Means of Grace taught and believed by Lutherans.

331. What is a sacrament?

A sacrament is a holy act, instituted by Christ, in which by visible means, He gives and confirms His invisible grace.

332. What are the sacraments of the New Testament?

The sacraments of the New Testament are Baptism and the Lord's Supper.

333. What were the rites of the Old Testament which foreshadowed the sacraments of the New Testament?

The rites of the Old Testament which foreshadowed the sacraments of the New Testament were Circumcision and the Passover meal.

The Sacrament of Baptism

334. What does the word baptism mean?

The English word *baptism* comes from a word in the Greek language which means a cleansing by washing, immersion, and/or a death.

335. What command about baptism has God given to His followers?

It is the word of Christ in Matthew 28:18-20, "All authority in heaven and on earth has been given to me. Therefore go and make disciples of all nations, baptizing them in the name of the Father and of the Son and of the Holy Spirit, and teaching them to obey everything I have commanded you. And surely I am with you always, to the very end of the age."

336. How is this baptism different from that of John the Baptist?

The baptism of John the Baptist was a baptism of repentance. In Christian Baptism, God gives the Holy Spirit.
Matthew 3:11 — *"I [John] baptize you with water for repentance. But after me will come one who is more powerful than I, whose sandals I am not fit to carry. He will baptize you with the Holy Spirit..."*

337. What does John the Baptist mean when He says that Jesus will baptize with the Holy Spirit?

He means that whoever is baptized by the authority of Jesus receives the Holy Spirit.
Acts 2:38 — *Then Peter said to them, "Repent, and let every one of you be baptized in the name of Jesus Christ for the remission of sins; and you shall receive the gift of the Holy Spirit"* (New King James Version).

338. What is Baptism?

Baptism is not merely water, but it is water used according to God's command and connected with God's Word.

339. What does it mean to be baptized in the name of the Father and of the Son and of the Holy Spirit?

It means that I have been brought into union with the Triune God, that I belong to Him, and that I bear His name.

340. Who should be baptized?

Everyone should be baptized because everyone needs the grace of God, including little children.
Matthew 28:19 — *"...Go and make disciples of all nations..."*

341. Why should little children be baptized?

1. They are helpless and therefore the ideal people for salvation.
Luke 18:15-17 — *People were also bringing babies to Jesus to have him touch them. When the disciples saw this, they rebuked them. But Jesus called the children to him and said, "Let the little children come to me, and do not hinder them, for the kingdom of God belongs to such as these. I tell you the truth, anyone who will not receive the kingdom of God like a little child will never enter it."*

2. They are sinners and need the grace of God.
Psalm 51:5 — *Surely I was sinful at birth, sinful from the time my mother conceived me.*

3. They are capable of receiving the blessings of baptism.
Mark 10:15,16 — *"...I tell you the truth, anyone who will not receive the kingdom of God like a little child will never enter it." And he took the children in his arms, put his hands on them and blessed them.*

4. They are capable of believing.
Matthew 18:6 — *"...These little ones...believe in me..."*

5. They are included in Jesus' command to "go into all nations."
Matthew 28:19,20a — *"Therefore go and make disciples of all nations, baptizing them in the name of the Father and of the Son and of the Holy Spirit, and teaching them to obey everything I have commanded you..."*
Acts 2:39 — *The promise is for you and your children...*

6. They were included in the Old Testament and therefore would not be excluded in the New Testament unless plainly forbidden (Colossians 2:11,12).

7. The early church sets the example by baptizing entire households, which certainly must have included little children (Acts 16:15,33; I Corinthians 1:16).

342. Can little children have faith?

Yes, little children can have faith because Jesus says that they believe (Matthew 18:6).

343. Are baptized children saved?

Yes, baptized children are saved because Jesus has given each one of them the gift of faith, and they do not resist Him by unbelief.

344. How shall these baptized children be regarded?

They shall be regarded as children of God and encouraged to take their sins to Jesus and choose daily to follow Him.

345. Are little children who have not been baptized condemned?

The Bible does not speak clearly about this. But we have the words of Jesus who said that our "...Father in heaven is not willing that any of these little ones should be lost" (Matthew 18:14).

346. When should an adult be baptized?

An adult who has never been baptized should be baptized only after confessing that Jesus Christ is Lord and Savior.

347. Should adults who were baptized as children but later leave the faith be rebaptized when they repent and return to faith?

No, to be rebaptized is to deny the promise of God given in baptism and which He has not taken back. Repentant persons simply return to the grace God gave them in baptism.

348. How is the faith of adults different from the faith given to little children by Christ?

They are not different since both are saving faith created by the power of God. However, adults are able to reflect on and think about their faith.

349. Who should baptize?

The church baptizes through its pastor unless there is an emergency when anyone should baptize.
I Corinthians 4:1 — *So then, men ought to regard us as servants of Christ and as those entrusted with the secret things of God.*

John 20:22,23 — *And with that he breathed on them and said "Receive the Holy Spirit. If you forgive anyone his sins, they are forgiven; if you do not forgive them, they are not forgiven."*

350. How are we to baptize?

No instruction is given in the Bible about how much water should be used or how it should be applied, only that we are to baptize in the name of the Father and the Son and the Holy Spirit.

351. What benefits did you receive when you were baptized?

1. My sin was forgiven.
Acts 2:38,39 — *Then Peter said to them, "Repent, and let every one of you be baptized in the name of Jesus Christ for the remission of sins; and you shall receive the gift of the Holy Spirit. For the promise is to you and to your children, and to all who are afar off, as many as the Lord our God will call" (New King James Version).*

2. I was born again.
John 3:3,5 — *...Jesus declared, "I tell you the truth, no one can see the kingdom of God unless he is born again." ...Jesus answered, "I tell you the truth, no one can enter the kingdom of God unless he is born of water and the Spirit..."*
I Peter 3:20b,21a — *In it [the Ark] only a few people, eight in all, were saved through water, and this water symbolizes baptism that now saves you also — not the removal of dirt from the body but the pledge of a good conscience toward God.*
Mark 16:16 — *"Whoever believes and is baptized will be saved, but whoever does not believe will be condemned."*
Titus 3:4-7 — *...When the kindness and love of God our Savior appeared, he saved us, not because of righteous things we had done, but because of his mercy. He saved us through the washing of rebirth and renewal by the Holy Spirit, whom he poured out on us generously through Jesus Christ our Savior, so that, having been justified by his grace, we might become heirs having the hope of eternal life.*

3. God adopted me into His family, the church.
John 1:12 — *...To all who received him, to those who believed in his name, he gave the right to become children of God.*

I Corinthians 12:12,13 — *The body is a unit, though it is made up of many parts; and though all its parts are many, they form one body. So it is with Christ. For we were all baptized by one Spirit into one body — whether Jews or Greeks, slave or free — and we were all given the one Spirit to drink.*

4. God established His covenant with me.

Colossians 2:10,12 — *...You have been given fullness in Christ ... having been buried with him in baptism and raised with him through your faith in the power of God, who raised him from the dead.*

Galatians 3:26-29 — *You are all sons of God through faith in Christ Jesus, for all of you who were baptized into Christ have clothed yourselves with Christ. There is neither Jew nor Greek, slave nor free, male nor female, for you are all one in Christ Jesus. If you belong to Christ, then you are Abraham's seed, and heirs according to the promise.*

5. God gave me a way to live.

Romans 6:1-4 — *What shall we say, then? Shall we go on sinning so that grace may increase? By no means! We died to sin; how can we live in it any longer? Or don't you know that all of us who were baptized into Christ Jesus were baptized into his death? We were therefore buried with him through baptism into death in order that, just as Christ was raised from the dead through the glory of the Father, we too may live a new life.*

352. How can baptism bring forgiveness of sins when Jesus is our only Savior?

The same Word of God that tells us that Jesus is our only Savior tells us also that baptism saves us. Therefore, we see that baptism is a means of grace through which Christ forgives us our sins (Mark 16:16; I Peter 3:20,21; Galatians 3:27).

353. How can water do such great things?

Water used in baptism does not do anything by itself because it is ordinary water. However, when this water is joined to the Word of God and used according to the command of Christ, it is Christian Baptism, and it becomes the gracious water of life as

St. Paul writes to Titus, "He saved us, not because of righteous things we had done, but because of his mercy. He saved us through the washing of rebirth and renewal by the Holy Spirit, whom he poured out on us generously through Jesus Christ our Savior..." (Titus 3:5,6).

354. What is the meaning of baptism with water?

Baptism with water means that we have been identified with Christ by being "...buried with him through baptism into death in order that, just as Christ was raised from the dead through the glory of the Father, we too may live a new life" (Romans 6:4).

355. How can you be kept in fellowship with God after baptism?

I am kept in fellowship with God only through the power of the Holy Spirit, who lives within me and ministers to me through Word and Sacrament.

John 14:26,27 — *"...The Counselor, the Holy Spirit, whom the Father will send in my name, will teach you all things and will remind you of everything I have said to you. Peace I leave with you; my peace I give you. I do not give to you as the world gives. Do not let your hearts be troubled and do not be afraid."*

Philippians 1:3,6 — *I thank my God every time I remember you ... being confident of this, that he who began a good work in you will carry it on to completion until the day of Christ Jesus.*

Colossians 2:6,7 — *So then, just as you received Christ Jesus as Lord, continue to live in him, rooted and built up in him, strengthened in the faith as you were taught, and overflowing with thankfulness.*

356. How does the Holy Spirit use the Word and Sacrament to keep you?

The Holy Spirit keeps me by helping me to see my sin and helping me to see more clearly what Christ has done for me.

357. Can a baptized person fall away from God?

Yes, a baptized person can fall away from God by resisting or ignoring the Holy Spirit and by neglecting prayer, the Bible, and the Lord's Supper.

I Timothy 1:18b,19a —...*Fight the good fight, holding on to faith and a good conscience.*

II Timothy 4:3,4 — *For the time will come when men will not put up with sound doctrine. Instead, to suit their own desires, they will gather around them a great number of teachers to say what their itching ears want to hear. They will turn their ears away from the truth and turn aside to myths.*

Hebrews 3:12 — *Take care, brethren, lest there be in any of you an evil, unbelieving heart, leading you to fall away from the living God (Revised Standard Version).*

358. How does the Holy Spirit restore the person who has fallen from baptismal grace?

The Holy Spirit restores all those who repent of sin and believe the promises that God has given.

I John 1:9 — *If we confess our sins, he is faithful and just and will forgive us our sins and purify us from all unrighteousness.*

Isaiah 55:6,7 — *Seek the Lord while he may be found; call on him while he is near. Let the wicked forsake his way and the evil man his thoughts. Let him turn to the Lord, and he will have mercy on him, and to our God, for he will freely pardon.*

Revelation 3:20 — *"Here I am! I stand at the door and knock. If anyone hears my voice and opens the door, I will come in and eat with him, and he with me."*

359. Must this person be baptized again?

No, God has not gone back on His Word. By confession of sin a person may return to fellowship with God.

Romans 3:3,4a — *What if some did not have faith? Will their lack of faith nullify God's faithfulness? Not at all!*

360. May your baptism serve to comfort you and strengthen you in your faith?

Yes, since my baptism stands firm on God's part, I know that he will joyfully receive me when I come to Him in repentance.

Luke 15:20 — *"...He got up and went to his father. But while he was still a long way off, his father saw him and was filled with compassion for him; he ran to his son, threw his arms around him and kissed him."*

361. What should be your attitude toward your baptism?

My attitude should be one of thanksgiving to God for giving me a salvation that is so free that I do absolutely nothing to earn it or deserve it.

362. How should parents, sponsors and members of the congregation show their love for baptized children?

1. By being a good example in Christian living.
Titus 2:7,8 — *In everything set them an example by doing what is good. In your teaching show integrity, seriousness and soundness of speech that cannot be condemned, so that those who oppose you may be ashamed because they have nothing bad to say about us.*

2. By praying for them.
I Timothy 2:1,3,4 — *I urge, then, first of all, that requests, prayers, intercession and thanksgiving be made for everyone ... This is good, and pleases God our Savior, who wants all men to be saved and come to a knowledge of the truth.*

3. By giving kind counsel and encouragement to them.
Ephesians 6:4 — *Fathers, do not exasperate your children; instead, bring them up in the training and instruction of the Lord.*

4. By providing for their instruction in the Word of God.
Matthew 28:19,20 — *"...Go and make disciples...baptizing them...and teaching them to obey everything I have commanded you."*

363. Does baptism depend in any way upon the person who does the baptizing?

No, baptism depends upon the Word of God and the promise connected to it. Baptism in no way depends upon the character or faith of the one who baptizes.

The Sacrament of The Lord's Supper

364. What is the sacrament of the Lord's Supper?

The Lord's Supper, instituted by our Lord Jesus Christ, is His true body and blood, in, with and under the bread and wine, given to Christians to eat and to drink.

365. Where is this written?

This is written in the Gospels according to Saints Matthew, Mark, and Luke and also by Saint Paul who said: "The Lord Jesus, on the night he was betrayed, took bread, and when he had given thanks, he broke it and said, 'This is my body, which is for you; do this in remembrance of me.' In the same way, after supper he took the cup, saying, 'This cup is the new covenant in my blood; do this, whenever you drink it, in remembrance of me'"

366. When did the Lord Jesus bring His Holy Supper into being?

Jesus brought His Holy Supper into being on the same night that he celebrated His last Passover with the disciples, was betrayed by Judas, and was turned over to His enemies to be crucified.

367. Is the Lord's Supper known by any other names?

Yes, sometimes it is called Holy Communion because it brings us into close union with Christ and with one another. Sometimes this sacrament is called the *eucharist* (thanksgiving) because we are thankful for the gift God gives us in this sacrament.

I Corinthians 10:16,17 — *The cup of blessing which we bless, is it not the communion of the blood of Christ? The bread which we break, is it not the communion of the body of Christ? For we, though many, are one bread and one body; for we all partake of that one bread (New King James Version).*

368. What do you receive when you take part in the Lord's Supper?

In, with and under the bread and wine, I receive the body and blood of Jesus Christ which He gave for me.

369. How do you know this?

I know this from Christ's own words when He said of the bread, "...This is my body..." and of the wine, "This is my blood..." (Mark 14:22-24).

370. What makes the bread and wine a sacrament?

God's own word, which is connected to the bread and wine, makes it a sacrament.

371. Does the bread and wine change into something different?

No, the bread continues to be bread, and the wine continues to be wine. The bread and wine, however, become the means Jesus uses to give me His true body and blood. I cannot explain this miracle, but because Jesus says that this is true, I believe it and accept it by faith. We Lutherans call this the doctrine of the Real Presence.

372. For whom is the Lord's Supper intended?

The Lord's Supper is intended only for believers in Jesus who are old enough to be taught and who can examine themselves.
I Corinthians 11:27-29 — *Therefore, whoever eats the bread or drinks the cup of the Lord in an unworthy manner will be guilty of sinning against the body and blood of the Lord. A man ought to examine himself before he eats of the bread and drinks of this cup. For anyone who eats and drinks without recognizing the body of the Lord eats and drinks judgment on himself.*

373. What benefits do you as a believer receive from the Lord's Supper?

When I worthily receive the Lord's Supper, I receive forgiveness of sin; I enter into a closer fellowship with Christ my Savior, and I am strengthened in faith, hope and love.

Matthew 26:27,28 — *Then he took the cup, gave thanks and offered it to them, saying, "Drink from it, all of you. This is my blood of the covenant, which is poured out for many for the forgiveness of sins..."*

374. How can physical eating and drinking produce such great benefits for you?

It is not the physical eating and drinking which bring great benefits but Jesus' own words of promise and assurance.

375. How may I receive the Lord's Supper worthily?

I am truly worthy and well prepared when I believe the words of promise and assurance spoken by my Savior.

376. How would I receive the Lord's Supper unworthily?

I receive it unworthily when I do not believe the words spoken by Jesus, when I am not willing to forgive those who have sinned against me, and when I receive the Lord's Supper only out of habit.

377. Why do some people neglect the Lord's Supper?

Some people neglect the Lord's Supper because they do not recognize the benefits which Jesus offers.

378. What will help you partake of the Lord's Supper worthily?

I will be helped to do so if I prayerfully examine my heart before God, confess my sins, admit my need of Jesus, and have an honest intention to give up even my most cherished sins.
I Corinthians 11:28,29 —*A man ought to examine himself before he eats of the bread and drinks of the cup. For anyone who eats and drinks without recognizing the body of the Lord eats and drinks judgment on himself.*
Psalm 139:23,24 — *Search me, O God, and know my heart; test me and know my anxious thoughts. See if there is any offensive way in me, and lead me in the way everlasting.*

379. Should you stay away from the Lord's Supper if you feel unworthy?

No, a sense of unworthiness is proper if it leads me to reach out for the worthiness of Jesus.

Matthew 5:3,6 — *"Blessed are the poor in spirit, for theirs is the kingdom of heaven...Blessed are those who hunger and thirst for righteousness, for they will be filled."*

380. What should your attitude be as you eat the bread and drink the wine?

My attitude should be one of grateful remembrance for the suffering and death of Jesus on the cross for me and for the grace given to me in the bread and wine.

Luke 22:19c — *"This is my body given for you; do this in remembrance of me."*

381. How should receiving Holy Communion affect your way of living?

Since I have received a holy gift from God in the Lord's Supper, I should live a holy life through the strength that Jesus gives.

Philippians 1:27a — *Whatever happens, conduct yourselves in a manner worthy of the gospel of Christ.*

I Peter 2:24 — *He himself bore our sins in his body on the tree, so that we might die to sins and live for righteousness; by his wounds you have been healed.*

Philippians 4:13 — *I can do everything through him who gives me strength.*

382. Why should you receive the Lord's Supper often?

I should receive the Lord's Supper often because of the kind command and promise of my Savior, and because of my own need of all God wants to give me on the basis of Jesus' sacrifice.

Conclusion of the Catechism

383. According to this catechism, who are you?

By God's grace, if I am a believer in and a follower of Jesus, I am a child of God.

John 1:12 — ...*To all who received him[Jesus], to those who believed in his name, he gave the right to become children of God...*

384. According to this catechism, where did you come from?

God allowed me to be conceived and watched over me even before my birth.

Psalm 139:14-16 — *I praise you because I am fearfully and wonderfully made; your works are wonderful, I know that full well. My frame was not hidden from you when I was made in the secret place. When I was woven together in the depths of the earth, your eyes saw my unformed body. All the days ordained for me were written in your book before one of them came to be.*

385. According to this catechism, why are you here on earth?

I am here to glorify God my Savior.

Isaiah 43:6b,7 — *Bring my sons from afar and my daughters from the ends of the earth — everyone who is called by my name, whom I created for my glory, whom I formed and made.*

Psalm 95:6,7 — *Come, let us bow down in worship, let us kneel before the Lord our Maker; for he is our God and we are the people of his pasture, the flock under his care.*

386. According to this catechism, if you believe in Jesus, where are you going?

Because of my Savior's resurrection, I have the hope of eternal life forever in the presence of God if I believe in Jesus.

John 11:25,26a — *"I am the resurrection and the life. He who belives in me will live, even though he dies; and whoever lives and belives in me will never die..."*

387. According to this catechism, how can you be sure of having eternal life and finally one day entering eternal life in heaven with God forever?

I can be sure of eternal life because of God's promise to me in the Scriptures.

John 20:31 —...*These are written that you may believe that Jesus is the Christ, the Son of God, and that by believing you may have life in his name.*

I John 5:11-15 — *This is the testimony: God has given us eternal life, and this life is in his Son. He who has the Son has life; he who does not have the Son of God does not have life.*

I write these things to you who belive in the name of the Son of God so that you may know that you have eternal life. This is the confidence we have in approaching God: that if we ask anything according to his will, he hears us. And if we know that he hears us — whatever we ask — we know that we have what we asked of him.

Scripture Text Index

Genesis
1:1 — 133
1:27,28 — 76, 81
2:2 — 49
2:18 — 76
3:8-10 — 146
3:15 — 149
3:17-19 — 146
3:19 — 307
8:21,22 — 149

Exodus
3:14 — 126
20:1-17 — 17-119
20:2 — 25
20:9-11 — 49

Leviticus
19:2b — 11
19:12 — 40
19:13 — 87
25:35 — 89

Numbers
23:19 — 126

Deuteronomy
6:4 — 128
6:13 — 39, 161

Nehemiah
9:17,31 — 126

Job
12:13 — 126
14:1 — 146

Psalms
8:1-9 — 148
8:3-9 — 56
19:1 — 125
19:7 — 108
23 — 192
23:5,6 — 229
40:1 — 283
46:10 — 292
50:10-12 — 103
50:15 — 45
51:5 — 112, 341
68:5,6 — 285
72:19 — 289
90:2 — 126
91:11 — 153
95:6,7 — 385
100:4 — 45
103:20 — 137
106:1 — 126
119:9,11 — 83,
  324, 326
119:105 — 21
122:1 — 292
125:2 — 26
139:13,14 — 56
139:17 — 1
139:23,24 — 378
145:15,16 — 152,
  304
145:17 — 126

Proverbs
1:10 — 319
3:5,6 — 33
8:13 — 31
14:34 — 65

17:15 — 92
19:5 — 92
25:18 — 92
28:13 — 214, 262
29:24 — 88
30:8,9 — 90, 304

Isaiah
1:18 — 226
6:3 — 126
9:6 — 161
9:6,7 — 172
29:13 — 250
42:1-3 — 220
42:21 — 108
43:6,7 — 385
43:25 — 226
53:5 — 224
53:6 — 211
53:7 — 190
55:6,7 — 212, 358
55:8,9 — 153
58:6,7 — 100
58:10 — 308
65:2 — 211
66:2 — 108

Jeremiah
29:11 — 153
33:3 — 283

Lamentations
3:22 — 110
5:7 — 110

Ezekiel
18:4 — 154

18:5,7 — 308

Daniel
12:2 — 269

Micah
2:1-2 — 98

Matthew
1:18-23 — 160
1:21 — 159
1:21 — 166
3:11 — 336
4:10 — 161
5:3,6 — 379
5:16 — 218
5:27,28 — 80
5:44,45 — 279
5:44 — 58
5:45 — 152, 304
6:6 — 278
6:9-13 — 273, 329
6:15 — 313
6:33 — 56
6:34 — 306
7:7 — 329
7:11 — 288
7:12 — 58
8:20 — 164
8:27 — 161
9:38 — 294
10:37 — 62
11:28,29 — 263
12:36,37 — 202
12:36 — 95
13:40-42 — 269
15:8,9 — 42
16:18,19 — 240
16:24 — 233
16:26 — 56
18:6 — 341, 342

18:14 — 345
18:15 — 95
18:15-17 — 255
18:18 — 252
18:21,22 — 314
19:4-6 — 75
19:8,9 — 78
22:37-40 — 23
24:4 — 204
24:6 — 204
24:7 — 204
24:36 — 203
24:44 — 203
25:35,36 — 235
25:40 — 106
25:41,46 — 268
26:27,28 — 373
26:36-46 — 188
26:41 — 326
27:46 — 188
28:1-10 — 161
28:18-20 — 161,
197, 200, 256,
335, 340, 341, 362

Mark
9:24 — 220
10:15,16 — 341
14:22-24 — 369
16:1-8 — 161
16:16 — 124, 351,
352

Luke
1:35 — 164
1:37 — 126
1:69,74,75 — 183
2:7 — 164
2:13,14 — 137
2:51 — 60
6:37 — 313

6:46 — 250
10:25-37 — 57, 69
10:27 — 18,23,27
11:28 — 7
12:15 — 90, 98
15:20 — 360
17:20-21 — 241,
293
18:15-17 — 294,
341
22:19 — 380
22:44 — 188
23:43 — 265
24 — 196
24:1-11 — 161
24:45-49 — 9

John
1:1,2,3,14,18 —
159, 161, 165
1:12,13 — 228,
351, 383
3:3-8 — 205, 230,
231, 295, 351
3:16,17 — 1, 118,
151, 155
3:18 — 177
3:36 — 157, 227,
270
4:24 — 126
5:23 — 161
5:24 — 5, 181
5:28,29 — 266
6:35 — 161
6:40 — 300
6:44 — 294
8:12 — 161
8:44 — 298
10:7 — 161
10:10 — 2
10:11 — 161

11:25,26 — 161, 266, 386
13:34,35 — 249, 302
14:1-4 — 101, 181, 201, 202
14:6 — 9, 161
14:21 — 32
14:26 — 206
14:26,27 — 355
15:1 — 161
15:7 — 281
16:7 — 242
16:13,14 — 7, 125, 215
16:24 — 276
17:3 — 130, 157, 217, 271
20:1-18 — 161
20:10-29 — 196
20:21-23 — 260, 349
20:28 — 161
20:30,31 — 3, 5, 125, 387
21:1-23 — 196
21:17 — 161

Acts
1:8 — 249, 256
1:11 — 198, 202
2:21 — 178
2:38,39 — 337, 341, 351
2:41,42 — 239
2:47 — 245
3:22 — 170
4:12 — 157, 270
5:29 — 62
10:38 — 168
13:38 — 260

16:15,33 — 341
16:30,31 — 178, 219
17:11 — 290
17:27 — 126
24:14 — 204

Romans
1:4 — 195
1:20 — 29, 125
2:4 — 210
2:14,15 — 17, 125
3:3,4 — 359
3:20 — 21, 209
3:23 — 19
4:25 — 195
5:1 — 229
5:1-5 — 223
5:5 — 229
5:10 — 119
5:12 — 112, 143
5:18 — 154
5:19 — 162
6:4 — 195, 354
6:1-4 — 351
6:14 — 180
6:23 — 181
8:1 — 227
8:5 — 322
8:7,8 — 146
8:9 — 238
8:11 — 266
8:15,17 — 223
8:22 — 147
8:26,27 — 274
8:28 — 153
8:33,34 — 171
10:17 — 52, 209, 231
12:1,2 — 259
12:4,5 — 238

12:5-8 — 258
12:13 — 100
13:14 — 249
14:5 — 51
14:17 — 293

I Corinthians
1:13 — 4
1:16 — 341
1:30 — 234
2:14 — 8, 146, 216
4:1 — 348
5:9-13 — 251
7:10,11 — 78
10:13 — 83, 326
10:16, 17 — 367
10:26 — 85
10:31 — 305
11:7-29 — 372
11:28,29 — 378
12:3 — 205
12:4-6 — 258
12:12,13 — 237, 351
13:4-7 — 95
15:1-5 — 12
15:3-9 — 196
15:20,21 — 195
15:33 — 82
15:42-44 — 267
15:51,52 — 266

II Corinthians
2:7,8 — 254
4:4 — 146, 216
5:15 — 183
5:17 — 228, 229
5:19,21 — 191
5:21 — 222
7:10 — 210
8:9 — 186

10:5 — 82
11:14 — 139
12:8,9 — 282

Galatians
2:16 — 19
3:10 — 117
3:13 — 180
3:24 — 21
3:26-29 — 351, 352
4:4,5 — 151, 162
4:6 — 286
4:8 — 128
5:16 — 249
5:19-21 — 99
6:1,2 — 95, 253

Ephesians
1:4 — 155
1:7 — 312
2:8-10 — 218, 222, 229, 295
2:14-18 — 16
2:19-22 — 238
3:9 — 161
3:14,15 — 132, 288
3:16-19 — 233
3:20,21 — 281
4:11-13 — 246, 258
4:22-24 — 228
4:25 — 93
4:28 — 89, 308
4:29-32 — 80, 93
5:3 — 80
5:19,20 — 305
5:23-25 — 77
6:1-3 — 59
6:4 — 362
6:10-12 — 138
6:12 — 303, 320
6:13 — 326

6:18 — 278, 287

Philippians
1:3,6 — 355
1:4,6 — 236
1:6 — 83
1:27 — 381
2:6,7 — 165
2:8 — 184, 190
2:12,13 — 232
2:13 — 83, 229
3:8,9 — 271
3:20,21 — 267, 325
4:8,9 — 82, 324
4:13 — 381
4:19 — 33

Colossians
1:13,14 — 179, 293
1:16 — 161
2:6,7 — 233, 355
2:9 — 160
2:10-12 — 341, 351
2:15 — 182
3:16 — 246

I Thessalonians
4:3-8 — 77, 300
4:16 — 202
5:17 — 278
5:23,24 — 232

II Thessalonians
2:3-8 — 204
2:14 — 209
3:10 — 307

I Timothy
1:8 — 20, 108
2:1,2 — 279
2:1,3,4 — 362

2:3-6 — 2, 294, 300
2:5,6 — 162
4:12 — 210
6:6 — 100, 107, 306
6:17 — 102
6:18 — 235

II Timothy
1:9 — 155
2:19 — 241
2:22 — 81
3:1-5 — 204
3:16,17 — 4, 236
4:3,4 — 357

Titus
1:16 — 250
2:7,8 — 362
2:11-14 — 303
2:13,14 — 161, 242
3:4-7 — 231, 351
3:5,6 — 353

Hebrews
1:1-6 — 149, 161
1:14 — 137
2:1,3 — 177
3:12,13 — 212, 357
7:18,19 — 16
7:25 — 312
7:27 — 171
9:12 — 163
9:24 — 198
10:24 — 235
10:25 — 52, 246
11:3 — 133
11:24,25 — 81
12:3 — 81
13:4 — 80
13:5 — 107

13:15,16 — 45, 69, 105
13:17 — 61

James
1:14-15 — 99, 321
1:17 — 305
1:27 — 52, 58
2:10 — 116
2:15-17 — 308
2:17 — 218
2:22 — 290
3:2 — 310
4:3 — 282
4:4 — 319
4:11 — 93
4:17 — 114
5:4 — 87
5:16 — 282

I Peter
1:3,5 — 101
1:18,19 — 174
1:23 — 231
2:11,12 — 249
2:24,25 — 236, 381
3:18,19 — 194
3:20,21 — 231, 351, 352
3:22 — 199
4:10,11 — 257, 290

II Peter
1:3,4 — 5
1:21 — 4
2:4 — 138
3:10-13 — 202
3:13,14 — 297

I John
1:6-10 — 214, 260, 261, 291, 315, 358
2:1,2 — 115, 176, 225, 311
2:15,16 — 319
3:2 — 180, 364
3:4 — 111
3:8 — 182, 298
3:10,11 — 249
3:15 — 67
3:16 — 69
3:17 — 89
3:20 — 126
4:16 — 126
4:19 — 229
5:11-15 — 311, 329, 387
5:20 — 161, 229

Revelation
3:20 — 358
11:15 — 202, 297
14:13 — 265
21:4 — 325
22:13 — 161
22:20 — 294

Subject Index

Abortion — 73
Adult baptism — 346
Adultery — 74-83
Amen — 272, 328
Angels — 137-138
Apostasy — 357
Apostles' Creed, The — 120-272
Ascension — 197-200
Backsliding — 357
Baptism — 334-363
Baptism, Adult — 346
Baptism, Benefits of — 351-354
Baptism, Infant — 341-344
Baptism, Mode of — 350
Baptism, Subjects of — 340-342
Bible — 1-12
Ceremonial Law — 14
Christ, Exaltation of — 193-205
Christ, Humiliation of — 185-192
Christ, Return of — 201-204
Christ, Suffering of — 185-192
Christian church — 237-260
Christian life — 249, 308
Christian membership — 248-250
Church discipline — 251-255
Church membership — 247-249
Church year — 53, 54
Civil Law — 14
Conjure — 35-45
Covetousness — 97-107

Creation, First Article of — 132-156
Creation — 132-136
Cursing — 35-45
Daily bread — 304-308
Death — 264-271
Divorce — 78
Enticements to evil — 316-326
Eternal death — 177
Eternal life — 271
Faith — 178, 218-221, 235, 342
Fall away — 357
Fall, The — 143-149
False witness — 91-96
Family life — 59-66
Father — 59-66
Forgiveness — 225-227
Forgiveness — 260-264, 309-315
Fornication — 74-83
Gifts — 258, 259
God — 126
God, Omnipotence of — 153
God, Preservation of — 152
God's will — 299-302
God's word — 1-12
Godparents — 362
Great Commission — 256-259
Hades — 193, 195
Hell — 193, 195
Holy Communion — 364-382
Holy Spirit — 206-272
Home — 59-66
Human nature — 321-323
Hypocrites- 250

Idolatry — 28-34
Image of God — 141-146
Incarnation — 164-165
Infant baptism — 341-344
Jesus Christ — 159-174
Jesus Christ is God — 161
Judgment — 270
Justification — 222-224
Keys of the kingdom — 252
Kingdom of God — 293-297
Law and Gospel — 11, 12
Lord's Prayer, The — 273-329
Lord's Supper — 364-382
Loving God — 27-54
Loving Others — 55-119
Lying — 91-96
Marriage — 74-83
Missions — 256-259
Moral Law — 15
Mother — 59-66
Murder — 67-73
New birth — 228-231
Oaths — 35-45
Office of the Keys — 252
Parents — 362
Parents — 59-66
Perjury — 35-45
Personal property — 85-90
Possessions — 102, 103
Prayer — 273-329
Preservation — 236
Property — 85-90
Real Presence — 371
Rebaptism — 347, 359
Redemption — 174-184
Redemption, Second Article of — 157-205
Repentance — 214, 260-264, 358
Resurrection — 195, 196

Resurrection of the body — 266-271
Return of Christ — 201-204
Revelation — 125
Sabbath — 46-54
Sacraments — 330-382
Sanctification — 232-235
Sanctification, Third Article of — 206-272
Sanctity of Life — 73
Satan — 139, 182, 298, 303, 318
Savior Promised — 150, 151
Second Coming — 201-204
Self-esteem — 55
Sin — 111-115
Slander — 91-96
Spiritual gifts — 258, 259
Sponsors — 362
Stealing — 85-90
Suicide — 70
Sunday — 46-54
Swearing — 35-45
Temptation — 82, 83, 316-326
Ten Commandments — 13-119
Testing — 316-326
Trespasses — 309-315
Trinity — 127-131
Truthfulness — 91-96
Will of God — 299-302
World — 319, 320